Izzie Firecracker and the Last of the Family Diamonds

Janet Butler Male

Published by Calmer Limited, 2017.

IZZIE FIRECRACKER AND THE LAST OF THE FAMILY DIAMONDS

First edition. November 26, 2017.

Written by Janet Butler Male.

For Mum and Dad

Forever missed

Martha, May 1996

MARTHA IS LANGUISHING in an outdoor hot tub, caressed by warm, soothing water. She's with her hunky husband, Randy, who wears only a Stetson and seductive grin. They are relaxing after a long and enjoyable day training horses.

'Working the ranch is one hell of a way to make money, honey,' says Randy in a gravelled drawl. 'I'd hate to work in an office.' He pours flutes of ice-cold Dom Perignon and hands one to his wife. 'Happy birthday, darling.'

Smiling into Randy's cognac-coloured eyes, Martha takes a sip of bubbly. She immediately spits out the nasty liquid - not champagne, but a mug of milky, weak tea. And she's not in a hot tub in Texas, but an avocado-coloured bath at home in Sussex, dreading another monotonous day.

Martha's staid and portly husband, James Hoare, not the honed, long-limbed Randy of her daydreams, comes into the bathroom, glorious in baggy y-fronts with a string vest. As he trims errant nostril hairs, he says, 'I know it's your birthday, that's why I made you a cuppa and let you have a half-hour lie-in, but get a move on as I need you in the office by nine o'clock. Don't be tardy.'

James isn't wearing a Stetson. The idea is laughable; a ten-gallon hat would look daft with his pinstripe suit. He finishes the nasal excavations then struts from the room as he says, 'Try and look presentable today; I wish you made more of an effort.'

Martha sticks out her tongue, visualising him in a pair of chaps, as silent revenge. Hmm, not a good look. The idea makes her giggle, offsetting her annoyance a tad.

Emerging from the bath, she feels rebellious. Damn it; she will lie in the watery cocoon for another five minutes. After adding more hot water, she rests back, closes her eyes, and returns to the hot tub, and sizzling man.

Randy's foot strokes her inner thigh, gradually moving higher. Burning lust overwhelms her. He draws nearer, skin to skin, the scent of earthy maleness drives her wild with desire. He whispers, 'Some ranch hands are hovering so I can't ravish you now, but we'll make up for it later.'

'I don't know if I can wait.' She yearns for his passionate sweet-scented kisses. Urgent with need, she reaches for his hard...

'Get out of that bath now! And you appear flushed; you must have the water too hot.'

Martha didn't hear James, now clad in a tight pinstripe suit, sneak into the room. He stomps out again, yelling, 'I'm going on ahead. See you at the office, get a bally move on.'

Reaching for a towel, she sings, 'Happy bloody birthday to me.'

Minutes later she yanks on the usual hateful uniform of shapeless tweed skirt, blouse and cardigan, before applying a quick slick of Peon Pink lipstick to her full mouth. It's impossible to be presentable with the horrid clothes, chosen by James. The irony makes her mad. She considers spraying a touch of her favourite perfume, l'Amour, to lift her spirits, but James complains it smells like a tart's boudoir. Most men would approve, but her husband is dull. Her entire life is staid and boring. She settles for a dab of the lavender oil which has the Hoare stamp of approval: 'If it was good enough for my mother, it's good enough for you. I won't have my wife smelling like a slut.'

'But you hated your mum.'

'That's not the point. At least Mother didn't smell like a loose woman.'

Martha should be having more fun, with spare funds for fripperies, and less time spent at work. They make plenty of money, but nearly every penny goes back into their estate agency business, or so James says. Any spare cash Martha has supports their son Simon's lazy lifestyle.

James won't accept their only child has a problem - Simon is a paragon. James hasn't realised that every time the offspring visits his beloved grandma in Los Angeles, he is a paying guest at the Dryout Spa in Palm Springs. He's been twice in the last year, with Martha's mum insisting on footing the hefty bills. Thank God.

Soon Martha is downstairs, brewing her first coffee of the day after pouring away the hideous tea. After all these years, James still can't make a cuppa the way she enjoys it - sweet and strong.

The doorbell rings. It must be Doris, the daily, back after a few weeks holiday in Cleethorpes. Much to Martha's surprise, Doris recently metamorphosed from dreary and downtrodden to radiant and confident. I must ask what her secret is, mulls Martha, opening the door.

A drunken Simon falls through it and throws up on the Chinese rug. What a stink!

'How did I get into this mess?' she mutters.

THE DOWNHILL SLIDE began when Martha was working in Wetherby's, an art auction house in Knightsbridge. It was her first job since she left school, Le Manoir, nicknamed Manners Manor, in Switzerland. She still recalls the shock on her mother's face when she landed home, a year later and fifteen pounds heavier than when she left: 'Oh, no, darling, it simply won't do. You're going on a diet.'

Swiss chocolate was impossible to resist. And the pastries for breakfast were a delightful contrast from the Spartan menu at her boarding school, Grimstone Academy for Girls. Martha shudders whenever she remembers the grey and lumpy porridge that heralded the start of a school day.

The young James bewitched Martha when he first popped into the auction house, over twenty years ago, interested in a painting. He was slim back then, his pinstripe suit falling elegantly, rather than straining over a pot-belly, and his hair was thick and dark, not grey and sparse. None of this would matter if James were nice to her, but he is horrid. And his initial sense of humour absconded without a trace long ago.

James asked her out for dinner straight away, and they enjoyed a delightful evening at The Holly in Covent Garden. He wanted to celebrate finding the girl of his dreams. He said he couldn't believe it when he came into Wetherby's and spotted his perfect woman, who reminded him of a young Kate Hepburn. Martha adored her in *Holiday*, in which she played the eccentric rich girl, Linda Seton. The latter elopes with Johnny Case, played by Cary Grant, and escapes her stuffy life in a Park

Avenue Mansion. Martha wishes she could run away from her oppressive life with James.

THE FIRST WEEKS AFTER they met were a whirlwind of fun and romance. For once Martha's experience was genuine, not an image on a screen or nestled within the pages of a book. She thought she might explode with happiness when James phoned her at home one Thursday evening:

'I'm taking you to Paris this weekend. Pack a case and bring your passport, a posh frock and some sexy lingerie. I'll meet you after work tomorrow afternoon, and we'll go straight to the airport.'

Martha was in a dreamy daze as she packed her little blue Antler suitcase and like a sleepwalker as she boarded the plane. Was this it? Was he taking her to the city of lovers to propose? She barely dared hope.

'Tell me where we're staying,' she pleaded, amber eyes alight with anticipation, as they drank white wine and munched peanuts on the flight.

'No, I'm not spoiling the surprise. Be patient, Martha dearest.'

When the taxi pulled up at l'Hôtel Riche, on Avenue George V, Martha gasped. Such decadence. And things became even better.

A few hours later she was sat opposite James in Le Restaurant Posh Nosh on the Champs-Élysées, enjoying pink champagne from delicate flutes.

James left his chair, and Martha thought he was off to the loo, but he got down on one knee, took a small box out of his pocket, and opened it with a flourish.

'My darling, Martha, I want you to become a Hoare.'

The idea was outrageous. What a goddamn nerve. James wanted her to be his mistress, French style, where was the respect? Then she remembered his surname.

'Yes, I'd love to be a Hoare.' He wanted to marry her - hurrah!

'I thought we'd get away from riff-raff this weekend,' said a snooty middle-aged English woman on the next table to her uptight looking partner.

Martha and James were in convulsions of mirth as they ordered Crepes Suzette for pudding.

As they were having coffee, a man came into the restaurant selling red roses. James bought one for Martha and said, 'For my ravishing future wife.'

She still has the flower, pressed in a scrapbook; its heady scent long disappeared, along with the joy of James.

THEY WERE IN THEIR early twenties when they married, with three years to go until Martha came into a large inheritance, courtesy of her beloved dad. And as a wedding present, he bought them a house which they've since upgraded twice. Simon was born a year after they said their vows.

Martha liked their first home, a sweet little semi-detached. And she adored their second house - a four-bedroom Victorian villa. It had spacious rooms, high ceilings and large windows which let in plenty of light, gladdening her heart.

She hates where they live now, Murdstone Manor, in the village of Dyke on the outskirts of Brighton. It's a dark, vast, sprawling and gloomy house, built in the seventeenth century. The ceilings are low and beamed, and small windows make it a challenge for sunlight to enter. The place spooks Martha. As soon as she ventured through the front door, at the first viewing, her skin goose-pimpled and dread invaded her soul.

'Let's go,' she whispered when the owner limped from the room, to give them space to confer. 'It gives me the creeps. Lots of the rooms smell horrid, a decaying, musty and damp aroma. I've got a nasty feeling.'

'Don't be ridiculous, Martha; you're paranoid. We'll get this property for a song, for God's sake, the value will go up hugely, and we'd be insane to walk away. The owner is desperate to sell. She's seen a nursing home she likes, Heaven's Gate, in Hoving, but needs to move fast.'

'Not much chance of that.'

'Please be serious.'

'Oh, for goodness' sake, lighten up, James. I *am* serious; about not moving into this sinister, smelly horror.'

'You're a drama queen and watch too many of those old movies. Get a grip. There's a stable on the grounds; you could have a horse if you agree on buying the house. I know how much you loved Trigger.'

Martha's throat tightened, remembering her beloved stallion, who had died from colic a few years before. Every time she'd mentioned getting another horse James moaned about the expense. 'We could have bought a second home with the cost of the vet and farrier bills. And don't get me started on hay, feed and insurance.'

'The upkeep of your flash cars isn't exactly cheap,' Martha rallied.

'Don't argue. The cars are important for business, but a horse is a silly indulgence.'

Maybe it was time to do some equine bargaining. Martha knew she couldn't win the primary argument. James wanted the horrible house, and he'd persist until he got his way. So she might as well get something *she* wanted. 'Well, OK, James: If I have my horse, I'll agree to the house.'

Martha's intuition was confirmed the day they moved to their new abode. She had a horse she loved and a house she hated. She took ages deciding on her new steed, and ten years on still adores her choice. Arabesque is a beautiful chestnut Arabian mare with a fiery and feisty temperament, but exhilarating to ride.

JAMES WAS ATTENTIVE and pleasant when they first married. He drove an understated Saab and worked for Sherlock Homes; *let us do the detective work to find your perfect house.*

He'd known Martha would receive a large inheritance on her twenty-fifth birthday before he even set foot in Wetherby's.

A distant and jealous relative on her dad's side was in one of James's favourite drinking haunts one night. He was exuding drunken vitriol about being excluded from some family wealth. He ranted about what should have been his going to a silly female called Martha. It hadn't taken James much detective work to find out where the lucky recipient of the inheritance worked.

Courting Martha used up most of James's savings, and the trip to Paris and the ring cost a year's salary. His wife is pleasant enough and *quite* nice looking, but if it hadn't been for her money he'd have waited for someone more special. She's rather homely, a pale imitation of the divine Kate Hepburn. *Women are so easy to flatter.*

As soon as Martha's inheritance hit the joint bank account it started leaking out into a limited company of which James was, and is, sole director. He won the argument to call it James's Estates, making the point that Hoare's Homes or Estates might give the wrong idea. And if it was called Martha's people might word-associate it with vineyards and think it was a wine company. If only.

Martha was too exhausted looking after a hyperactive Simon to argue. James told her she was valuable in her role as Company Secretary. But he concealed her lack of shares.

First, he took control of her bank accounts; then he took control of her life.

Martha knows she's daft to put up with it, but over the years she's given away most of her power. James even accompanies her on the rare occasions she shops for clothes and acts like a top fashion advisor. It's a wonder Lady Di didn't ask him to design her wedding gown. Imagine it - *And here is the Princess now, emerging from the carriage in her sensible little Hoare dress. In case the weather turns chilly, she is carrying a hand-knitted cardigan.*

Martha has learned it's not worth the sulks if she shops without her husband's approval. He even hates it if she wears shoes with over a one-inch heel, because at five feet seven she's only slightly shorter than James. She should buy a pair with vertiginous heels, to spite him.

In her heart, she wants to live in jeans and cowboy boots and hates most of her clothes. They make her look like a stuffy spinster from an old movie: She is Charlotte Vale from *Now Voyager*, but the jailor is her husband instead of her mother. It would be wonderful if her life emulated the end of the movie, not the beginning. She visualises Randy. 'Why ask for the moon, Martha, when we have the stars?'

EVERY DAY, MARTHA TRIES to convince herself she's happy, despite the haunted house and gloomy husband. She's not and is sinking further into the doldrums because James has banned her from riding Arabesque since a recent accident. She should just get on her horse, giving James the finger as she gallops into the distance, but hasn't the energy or the stomach for more arguments.

After yet another horrible row with James, Martha slugged back one of the half bottles of gin she hides under the hay. Delirious, she went for a cross-country gallop and fell off while jumping a hedge. Arabesque wasn't hurt, but Martha spent a month in bed recovering from sprains, cracked ribs and a bruised ego.

James was furious because he had to use a temporary secretary. He hated the extra expense and worried the stand-in would spot the dodgy dealings he thinks his wife too stupid to notice.

Martha suspects he and the doctor collaborated on the riding ban. They are old mates, and she wonders if money and mutual back-scratching were involved. She berates herself; I am Martha, the Martyr - too worn down to defy orders.

James says that as she spends so much money on her horse, it entitles him to a decent car - or two. So while poor Martha drives to and from PriceChoppers supermarket in her battered old Volvo estate, James speeds around the country visiting properties in his Porsche or Range Rover. Everything is for him.

Recently she tried to revive their extinct romance. When James was watching the news, she slinked into the room in a low-cut diaphanous short black silk nightgown, stockings, suspenders and high heels.

'Martha, you're blocking the telly and look ridiculous. You'll catch your death of cold, and then who will look after the office when I'm out looking for deals? Put on a warm flannelette nightdress.'

The next day she took the silk number to a charity shop.

MARTHA LIKES SHOPPING for food and cooking it - the only area of her life she has freedom. James doesn't object as she is a superb cook, due to the cordon bleu course she received as a twenty-first birthday present from her parents.

His burgeoning tummy is a testament to his love of her puddings, which Martha always resists, not wishing to lose her figure and last vestiges of pride. The horrified expression on her mother's face when she got back from Switzerland stops her overeating to this day.

James doesn't let her drive his cars. 'They're too fast for you darling; I am so worried you'll kill yourself and I do love you.'

What a pile of horseshit, Martha rages, shovelling muck in the stable, and visualising chucking it over his smug head. She is experiencing the drudges and none of the delights of her horse. But at least Simon keeps Arabesque exercised; he rides to blow away the cobwebs when he has a hangover. The amount of alcohol her son drinks, it's a wonder the poor horse hasn't dropped dead from exhaustion or alcohol fumes.

James does not understand what a mistake he makes in thinking his wife stupid.

The doorbell rings again.

The transformation of Doris

MARTHA OPENS THE DOOR, having moved the smelly rug to one side. 'Ah, hello, Doris, welcome back. Wow, you look fantastic. Your hair is stunning. When did you go blonde? You must have lost another half stone, and you look ten years younger. And whose is the red convertible sports car in the drive? You've changed for the better in such a short time. How on earth have you done it?'

Doris takes off her coat and hat then smoothes her chin-length bob. 'Steady on, one thing at a time. Let's have a cup of coffee, and I'll tell you.'

'I'd love to, but I can't. James will go mad if I'm not in the office soon.'

'He can sod off; it's your birthday. I've brought some scrummy Danish pastries from Flour Power to have with our drinks, as a treat.'

'Yummy, thanks, I thought I caught a waft of vanilla as I opened the door, but the smell of Simon's vomit overwhelmed it, I'll go and clear it away.'

'No, you won't, he can do it himself.' Doris marches to the foot of the stairs, and shouts, 'Simon, come downstairs and clean your disgusting mess.'

At first, Martha is outraged at her cleaner's audacity. Then she grins and feels a small ray of hope, like the sun coming out after an endless winter.

Doris takes a sip of coffee. 'Ooh, I needed that! Thanks for noticing my new appearance,' she says, batting beautifully made-up hazel eyes. 'I was sick of that mousy brown home dye, covering the grey, so took the plunge and went to a posh salon and asked for honey blonde. I feel six feet tall instead of my usual five foot two.'

'I should take a leaf out of your book, Doris, and treat myself to a new hairdo. I've got more grey than auburn, these days. Come on, tell me more.'

'Do you remember when I used to turn up here on the bus to do the cleaning? Did you think it was because we didn't have a car?'

'It never even crossed my mind.'

'Well, it wasn't. Benny owned a grey Morris Minor for years, but we only used it on Sundays.'

Martha pauses after taking a bite of tasty pastry. 'Why only on Sundays, was Mr Minor religious?'

'Ha ha! When I was a kid, Mum made us keep our best clothes and shoes for high days and holidays. Benny took the same view with the car and saved it for weekends. He worried the precious vehicle would get scratched, and left it in the garage during the week, and pedalled to work on his bike. The car stayed in the garage, even on rainy days. Benny was so careful with everything he was barely alive.'

'Wow, Doris, he makes me sound liberated.'

'The poor lamb was sick with worry if he veered from any of his routines. It wasn't only the car he fretted about; it was

lots of things. He was scared to go to the newsagent to buy a paper unless he had the exact money. Once, when he didn't know
the price of the Daily Wail had gone up, he came back, without
it.'

'Didn't he have any other money with him?' asks Martha.

'Yes, but waiting for change was outside his routine and
safety zone.'

'Blimey, and I thought I had problems.'

'We holidayed in the same caravan park in Bognor every
August for nearly thirty bleeding years because he was frightened to try anywhere else. This year we're off to Lanzarote and
can't wait. Our tea menu at home was the same each week.
Oh, it's Tuesday, must be egg and chips. My son planned visits
on Wednesdays, steak night. Our daughter chose Fridays for
corned beef hash. I was blinking sick of it. We never had my
favourite, steak and kidney pudding. I was a fool.'

'Who devised the exciting bill of fare, Doris?'

'His mum did when the kids were little; she thought not
having to worry about food would make life easier. It was the
same shopping list every week. When we married, Benny told
me he wanted to carry on with the same menu, and I was too
daft and starry-eyed to argue.'

'Sounds insane, but I'm in no position to pass judgement.
How does this relate to your transformation?'

'Everything - I was living his life and not my own. I could
talk to Benny until I was blue in the face but nothing convinced
him. It was only when Izzie Firecracker told me it's a waste of
energy trying to change someone, you have to change yourself
that things began to improve. Thank the Lord.'

'Who's Izzie Firecracker?'

'My angel, she helped turn my life around. When I became myself, Benny came out of his shell, and his stifling routine and rules. The sports car is his, not mine. And last night he told me he hates corned beef hash. Well, I suppose I should get on, the house won't clean itself. But I'm sorry love; I still can't go into the bedroom and bathroom at the end of the downstairs corridor on my own, those rooms give me the collywobbles.'

'Me too, Doris, we've stopped using them. Luckily the house is big, so there's still enough space. Even James won't go in the rooms I hate, although he won't admit they're creepy.'

'What excuse does he give, then?'

'He says the rooms are chilly, even in summer, but, of course, that can be a classic sign of an unwanted presence.' Chills run up Martha's back. 'But James insists the coldness is simply due to lack of insulation: Tosh!'

A FRIEND VISITED WITH her Great Dane, Scooby. Linda pooh-poohed the suggestion the house was creepy and announced that she and the pooch would spend the night in the Horror Wing:

The next morning, at breakfast, Linda was chalk-white and clutched her mug of tea as if it were a talisman. 'That was the worst experience of my life, Martha - I was terrified and should have listened to you.'

'Why didn't you move to another part of the house? There are plenty of rooms.'

'I did, after five minutes. I couldn't stay another moment after what I saw.'

'What did you see?'

'I can never speak of it; it was too awful.'

Ropes of terror curled tightly around Martha's tummy, but she clung to a phantom of hope. 'But if Scooby accompanied you, it must be OK; dogs are renowned for sensing negative vibes.'

'Are you kidding? As soon as we entered the corridor, my brave pooch whimpered then turned tail and ran back into the kitchen. I've never seen him move so fast, not even for a biscuit.'

'YOU LOOK MILES AWAY, Martha. Are you OK?' asks Doris.

'I hate this spooky house and must tackle James about selling it. He's waiting for it to go up in value, after the current slump. He wants to make a killing, ironic, as I can't help feel there was a grisly murder here.'

'Stop it, Martha, or I'll leave before I even start work and never come back. Go to the office, and I'll get on with my dusting. I'll avoid the Horror Wing and turn on the radio to keep me company. Terry Wogan made me laugh yesterday morning when a school dinner lady phoned in at eight o'clock. He told her she'd better get off the phone and into work as she only had a few hours left to overcook the cabbage. Gran used to do that, and the smell was disgusting.'

Martha laughs. 'I loved a few of the school meals, cheese pie was my favourite, but others were dreadful. We had a bully of a dinner lady at my junior school, Miss Harrigan, who wore a furry hat all day, every day, even in summer; she probably didn't even take it off at bedtime. Anyway, Harrigan the Harridan always made us eat every bite of lunch. It was lumpy mashed potato or semolina I dreaded the most. Were there any meals you loved or hated, Doris?'

'I detested the pink custard, ever since a horrid boy told me the main ingredient was human blood. Yuk! I'm getting you back for talking about murders. It's fine for you; you're off out. I've got to stay here on my own.'

'Sorry to frighten you Doris, but I was so relieved when you first came to work here and said you found the house spooky. I often wondered if I was going mad, or James was deliberately driving me crazy, like the husband in *Gaslight*, with Ingrid Bergman.'

'You and your old movies, I prefer my soaps. I love *Coronation Street* and *East Enders*, never miss them. Enjoy the rest of your birthday and don't let James bully you, stand up for yourself.'

'I'd like to be brave; James pushing me around drives me nuts. Tell me more about Izzie Firecracker next time. I'm intrigued.' Heading to get her coat she shouts, 'Simon, get downstairs right this minute now and clean up your disgusting mess.'

Carlotta Ricci, May 1996

CARLOTTA RICCI HEARS a tap at her study door, followed by the sounds of it squeaking open and soft footsteps. Wolf Song pads in on suede moccasins, proffering a cup of hot water and a dry rice cake - yummy!

I'd love a mug of tea and a bacon sandwich she daydreams, dragging her eyes from the computer screen and bidding Wolf a good morning. He always gets up a few hours later than she; the lazy sod.

'Did you sleep well, Wolf?' she asks, trying her best not to laugh.

Wolf Song used to be plain old Colin Cooper, but he changed his name in a shamanic ceremony a few months ago.

Wolf gives an exaggerated yawn. 'No, I didn't. I'll never get a proper night's sleep unless we move. The house faces the wrong way, and I can't align the bed so my head points in the exact right direction. I don't understand why you ignore all the principles of feng shui.'

'You're welcome to design the perfect abode if you want to pay for it. Until then I'm staying here. I'm sorry the way it faces doesn't suit you. Generations of miners have lived in this sweet terraced house. I've always loved it, that's why Granny left it to me.'

'If I were the one with the money, I'd live wherever you wanted. I like to put other people first.' Wolf performs his usual trick of making out he is the generous one and Carlotta the mean one in the relationship. In fact, he doesn't contribute a penny, and she pays for everything. It has been this way for five years, ever since they met in the mud at Glastonbury, and Colin's makeshift tent, made from old sheets, blew away in a strong gust of wind. Carlotta came to the rescue and let him share her cosy wigwam.

Wolf senses the hostile atmosphere and changes the subject. 'Do you fancy brown or green lentils for lunch? Let me know within the next five minutes as I need to soak them. But don't interrupt me when I'm doing my yoga, or it might spoil my energy for the day.' He ambles from the room, with what he assumes is an inconspicuous admiring glance in the mirror. Since someone told him he was the spit of Johnny Depp, in *Don Juan DeMarco*, he's been applying eyeliner and is always checking it hasn't smudged.

Carlotta rages with resentment as her internal Wolf Song dialogue goes into overdrive: The lazy, silly git. What energy? He'll be wearing an eye mask and cape next. Where is this 'money' I'm supposed to have? I barely scrape by on my income as it is. And I must have more protein besides those flippin' lentils. I'll nip into town, under a pretext. If I tell him the truth, I'll get disapproving and shocked looks for at least two days. He judges eating eggs as akin to cannibalism. Mum calls him the Food Police, and she's right. I'm a mug to put up with all his nonsense.'

Discarding cosy floral pyjamas, she takes a quick shower with her favourite grapefruit scented soap, then pulls on jeans, baggy sweatshirt and trainers. She notices the jeans are extra tight, and her tummy bulges over the waistband. They must have shrunk in the wash. Outside the living room, she pauses then taps on the door, to warn Wolf, before she enters. What is she doing, knocking to get permission to enter a room in her own home?

Wolf is standing on his head but pops himself the right way up, looking furious.

'I thought I asked you not to disturb me when I'm doing yoga?'

It's my effing lounge seethes Carlotta. 'I'm nipping into town as we are low on dates and figs. Don't worry about whether to soak green or brown lentils for lunch; either is fine. Enjoy your yoga, and I'll see you soon.'

IN HER FADED RED PANDA, driving to the local town of Pontingpool, Carlotta thinks; dried fruit, my arse. I'm off to my favourite cafe for a sausage and egg sandwich. I'll sit and enjoy it while I mull over what to do about Colin.

Arriving at the Crempog Cafe, aromas of bacon frying and coffee brewing are foreplay for Carlotta's deprived taste buds. The owner, Nerys, looks pleased to see her. 'Are you running away from Colin, I mean, Wolf, and his lentils, again?'

Nerys, a neighbour and friend, knows how Colin has inveigled himself into Carlotta's life. Even a saint has their limits, and she senses her mate has had more than enough.

'You guessed right. I want Colin to go, but I'm trapped.'

'No, you're not. You only think you are. You're only twenty-five, with your life ahead of you. A few sessions with Izzie Firecracker should sort you out. And you won't look back.'

'Who the heck is Izzie Firecracker?' Carlotta takes a sip of strong black tea. 'And where do I find her?'

'In London, she's a sort of unconventional therapist who's more like a good mate. She helped my sister, Angharad, turn her life around last year. Sis wanted a divorce, but she and the hubby are lovebirds these days. I'll find Izzie's details. Then I must get on with some cooking. Another chef has walked out, dratted prima donna!'

'I don't want to visit someone who persuades me to stay with Wolf.'

'No, she won't. Izzie helped my sister get to the crux of the matter; she didn't automatically agree when Angharad said she was ready to end the marriage. Sis enjoyed talking her problems and issues through with someone who had empathy but didn't judge. She said it was as if Izzie had taken her murky eyeglasses, polished them and added rosy, but clean lenses.'

'Then, yes, give me Izzie's details and a black coffee, please. Oh, and I'll have a chocolate croissant, for pudding, after my scrummy breakfast.'

BACK HOME, THOUGHTS of Wolf Song anger Carlotta. The more she dwells on the situation, the more of an idiot she feels. She spends most of her time stepping around his sensibilities, and why on earth can he not get a job?

'Colin, I mean, Wolf. It's a struggle to pay for everything without your help. I know your contribution is cooking lunch, but it doesn't pay the bills. Could you please get a job, even a part-time one?'

Apart from anything else, it would be bliss to have the house to herself more often. Carlotta loves it on the rare times he goes away to visit his sister in Leeds. It's a joy to avoid lentils for a few days and feast on treats such as fish and chips.

Wolf looks outraged. 'I have a job. I'm a poet. You're a writer. You should understand.'

Carlotta has a regular piece in the Daily Excess called Carlotta's Column, about how to get joy out of every day. If her readers knew what a hypocrite and pushover she is they'd never read it. She wants to write a novel but spends any spare energy resenting Wolf.

'You've not had a poem published since the mung bean one, years ago, in the Vegetarian News.'

'It's a good poem.' Wolf recites it for the millionth time.

ODE TO THE MUNG BEAN
    I'm a mung bean loving hippie
    And I think they are divine
    They taste good in risotto
    And you can have them with wine
    You can sprout them in a jar
    You can adore them from afar
    They burst with healthy nutrients
    There is not much on a par
    If you add them to a curry
    There is no need to worry
    They are kind to your digestion

And don't upset your tummy
So do yourself a favour
This bean you ought to savour
They're perfect for your health
Never leave them on the shelf

'YES, IT'S A SUPER POEM,' fibs Carlotta, 'But being a poet doesn't pay the electricity bill or the council tax. And if you didn't live with me, you'd have to pay rent or a mortgage.'

'Well, you'd have to pay for the electricity, council tax and stuff whether I lived here or not, and you don't even have a mortgage, you inherited this house. When I was at university, we all shared and shared alike. I'm the more generous person - if you couldn't sell your column, I wouldn't make you feel a failure. You're nasty! I'm going to cook lunch; it will be ready in an hour.' Wolf storms from the room, forgetting to glance in the mirror.

The meal is a sombre affair, with Wolf in yet another mood. It's like living with Kevin the Teenager. Carlotta is furious, poking at soggy lentils and overcooked vegetables: Why am I in this situation and why don't I ask him to leave? What the heck is wrong with me? I'm a pushover, but I'd feel mean throwing him out as his first refuge is no longer there because his parents both died within six months of each other, two years ago. Before then he used to flounce home to his childhood home in Manchester. I would dance around the house whenever I got back from dropping him at the train station. I never dance these days, not when I'm at home. My grandparents would cry if they knew what a dull and sad place their once happy home is nowadays.

CARLOTTA'S PARENTS are alive, well and living in Cardiff. They exude happiness, fun and passion when together, which makes her more depressed over her unfulfilling relationship with Wolf. Her mum, a geography teacher, has lived in Wales all her life, and her dad, a librarian, moved over from Italy when he was eighteen.

Carlotta enjoyed a lovely upbringing, and her parents are proud of their daughter, an only child. They never get bored with people remarking on her smooth olive-toned skin, large brown expressive eyes and curly dark hair. The only thing they were ever strict about was her name; her dad would not allow her to shorten it to 'Carly'.

'You were christened Carlotta; you are my beautiful reminder of Italy, my amore.'

Carlotta knows her mum and dad have little respect for Wolf. They are both hard workers and resent the lack of support given to their daughter.

When Carlotta has hinted at splitting up in the past, Wolf has got upset and told her how much he loves her; he tries his best and can't help the way he is. She's not sure. If she didn't support him, he'd have to change his ways – or starve, unless he found another gullible or lovestruck woman to support him.

Carlotta never truly loved Wolf but was in lust for the first six months. Her previous boyfriend was timid in the passion department. Wolf was wild and feral, to begin with, covering her body in musky hot kisses, making her shiver with want.

The relationship death knell sounded when she let him move in with her after she inherited the house, and he changed from wildcat to lazy cat. They don't even sleep in the same bed. Wolf proclaimed it drains his positive energy to share a room while sleeping. What positive energy, for Pete's sake?

She should have spent more time living alone, before letting Wolf become a permanent unwanted houseguest. Scratch that, he should never have gained admittance, but the hints were merciless and persistent, and she was weak after ending the relationship with her first love. Instinct said no at the outset; she wanted to spend more time enjoying the house, on her own. *If we can't enjoy aloneness, no one can thoroughly enjoy being with us*, her wise gran had said. Carlotta revels in solitude on the rare occasions Wolf leaves his den. But it was exciting at first. They had poetry, writing and a love of Pink Floyd in common, and were both vegans.

Neither of them has been vegan for a few years, due to their love of creamy milk chocolate. Carlotta isn't even vegetarian these days, but she doesn't dare tell Wolf. He has to go.

After lunch, Carlotta finds the piece of paper with Izzie Firecracker's number on it. Could this be her *Papillon* escape raft? She hopes the fees won't be too expensive. If they are, she has a nest egg in a secret bank account, from a recent win on the premium bonds. She told Wolf she'd won a mere fifty quid when it was a fabulous two thousand pounds.

Hang on a minute, what's that burning smell? She rushes into the living room to find Wolf snoring on the sofa; his joint has fallen out of his hand, setting a cushion alight. Carlotta runs to the kitchen sink, fills a bucket from the cold tap, dashes towards the fire and flings a torrent of ice-cold water over the inferno, successfully dousing the flames - and Wolf. Quel dommage!

Portia Belmont-Flowers, May 1996

WHEN PORTIA BELMONT was born, in 1967, her pretty mouth contained the proverbial silver spoon. She was brought up in a decadent house on Archdeacon Avenue, in North London, by adoring and indulgent parents. Holidays were in swanky hotels in the Caribbean or the Far East. Schools were private and boarding.

Boring, not boarding, she and her friends joked. They knew nothing but a privileged existence, so didn't appreciate it and longed for the glamour of grunge.

They ostentatiously tried to live a low-rent lifestyle, opting for dismal and damp dwellings while they were at university and in their first jobs, much to the contempt of fellow students and workers who were genuinely struggling.

The rich kids phoned their mummies and daddies when they tired of playing poverty. Going home to the family piles at weekends to feast on sumptuous meals and wallow in deep hot baths caused disdain from those who toiled in pizza parlours and the like, to pay for their education. One wit, working her way through university, jested that the only family piles her folks knew of were those requiring ample applications of haemorrhoid cream.

PORTIA SAILED THROUGH her degree and into a job at Connings Ad Agency on Regent Street. Life was fun, filled with parties and socialising, and she and her mates lived it up in decadent 80's London.

One night, in Bella's Nightclub, she met her soul mate, Todd. He was gorgeous and looked a little like James Dean. For a year she was in bliss, and then it fell apart when he visited his parents in the South of France. He zoomed off for a ride on his dad's motorbike and crashed into a wall, sustaining a nasty head trauma and falling into a coma. Portia rushed to see him, sitting for hours by his bed every day, praying for his recovery.

Todd gained consciousness six weeks later but couldn't remember her, and the doctor said it was no use, as he'd lost most of his faculties, and needed full-time care. His distraught parents begged her to stay away as her presence reminded them of how alive and vibrant their precious son had been. He couldn't even recall his mum and dad.

Portia's heart never recovered. She tried to revisit Todd, but his mum's tears on the phone made her feel guilty. She developed a cheerful veneer, with emptiness and despair lurking beneath the surface. Her rock-chick sexy outfits were history, and she dressed in Sloane Ranger style twinsets and pearls - from Marianne Faithfull to Lady Diana Spencer.

Connings sacked her; Portia's creativity died with the loss of Todd. Her worried parents checked her into the Friary, a private mental health hospital in Roebottom, north of London. It was expensive and exclusive. The rooms boasted luxurious four-poster beds and old-fashioned bell-pulls for service. The en-suite bathrooms had claw-foot baths and endless supplies of dazzling white fluffy towels. The pills arrived on silver salvers.

There, when she was twenty-three, she met her husband-to-be Fabian Flowers, a recovering alcoholic, in the communal lounge one evening. They got on well, and while together forgot their problems, finding their private chats more healing than group therapy.

The Friary imposed a strict lights-out policy at 10 pm, but Fabian and Portia carried on talking via the in-room telephones. They loved discussing their favourite childhood books and TV shows, often giggling way into the early hours at the exploits of *Terry and June*, *George and Mildred* and other nostalgic treats.

FABIAN'S FOLKS OWN a magnificent stately home in Sussex, Camberley Castle, and a large posh pad in Holland Park.

After they left the Friary, Portia stayed at Camberley Castle most weekends. On Tuesday and Thursday evenings she went for dinner or drinks with Fabian in London. The routine never varied. They were comfortable with each other because they met when they were both at their most vulnerable.

They didn't admit disappointment regarding their lacklustre physical relationship: From their first grope in Camberley's Royal Suite, where Victoria and Albert once stayed the night, the sex sucked. But they made each other feel secure, and although they got bored with each other, in bed and out of it, Fabian proposed and Portia accepted.

They married in St Paul's. Portia wore a sleek silk ivory sheath, by Catherine Donner, which flattered her slim five-foot-eight figure. She looked dazzling with her crystal-blue eyes and platinum blonde hair, worn in a chignon. A diamond tiara completed the vision of loveliness.

Her granny, resplendent in pink lace, declared her the most beautiful bride she'd seen since Grace Kelly married Prince Rainier. The proud parents dreamed of heirs and heiresses. Afterwards, there was a lavish reception in Parridges Hotel followed by a three-week honeymoon at the exclusive Sandy Beach resort in Barbados.

If the telling of this sounds flat, it's intentional. Portia has continued to feel sad for her entire marriage. No children have appeared, and she's glad. A friend who has a son is ecstatic he's the image of her hubby. Portia imagines having an offspring who resembles Fabian. The thought makes her feel sick. She'd want to slap a Fabian-like face. She weeps when she remembers how much she wanted a son who resembled her beautiful Todd.

Portia continues to find Fabian dull. For fun, he spends hours poring over his stamp collection and for work, helps manage the diverse family businesses.

Fabian hasn't reverted to alcohol and Portia is tempted to slip a measure or three of gin into his tonic water to see if he perks up: Some bedroom action might be better than the zero of the last few months. If it wasn't for her battery-operated friend, from Up all Night in Soho, she might as well check herself into the nearest convent.

AFTER A SHOPPING SPREE in Knightsbridge, their chauffeur doesn't arrive at the appointed time. A bus going in Portia's direction pulls up a few yards away, and she jumps on. It's packed, but she finds a seat next to an elegant woman, with cat-like green eyes and mid-brown hair. 'I love buses, don't you? I'm Izzie.'

Portia thinks it might sound snooty to say she's on public transport because the chauffeur was late. Instead, she asks, 'Have you been shopping?'

'No. I'm off to meet a friend. It looks like you've been enjoying retail therapy, though. I see you've been to Sloane's. I have a hard time finding stuff in there; it's a little too staid, I like a bit of drama and prefer the excitement and variety of the King's Road.'

'Sloane's is where I do most of my clothes shopping at the moment. My mum encouraged me to wear classic clothes in my teens; she's great fun, but her taste is conservative. I rebelled for a while and even used to travel to LA to buy funky stuff on Melrose Avenue. Now it's back to the uniform.'

'Do you enjoy them, the classic clothes?'

Portia's eyes fill with tears. 'No.'

Izzie rummages in a red velvet handbag and pulls out a small silver case, from which she extracts a card, handing it to Portia. 'This is my stop. I can help, if you want. Call me.' Then she wafts off the bus, leaving behind a heady fragrance of rose, amber and cinnamon.

Portia watches Izzie saunter on low-heeled red shoes with silver buckles. She wears black jeans with a red velvet fitted jacket, trimmed with black ostrich feathers at hem and cuffs. Her shoulder-length hair is behind the ears, with a cute red leopard print pillbox hat atop her head. She walks jauntily, holding her slim, about five-foot six frame high, and sports an amused smile, which suggests she finds the slightly eccentric clothes, and life in general, fun and not to be taken seriously. Portia wants some of that, and looks at the simple albeit elegant cream card, with thermo graphic raised print.

Izzie Firecracker
The Second Chance Club
Had enough?
It's time to take back control of your life

AT THE BACK OF THE card, there's a Mayfair phone number. A strong instinct makes Portia put it safely inside an inner zipped compartment of her handbag. She has a hazy memory she's seen Izzie before, but can't remember where or when.

As the bus pulls out of Sloane Square and drives past Peter Jones, Portia stands to let the driver know she wants to get off, and shouts, 'Stop here, my good man,' as she always instructs their chauffeur, as a joke. Realising the mistake, when the passengers look at her aghast, and some snigger, she can't get off quick enough.

'With pleasure, your Ladyship.' The driver applies the brakes, and the bus pulls to a halt outside Chelsea Barracks, and Portia hops off, red-faced, bumping into a Chelsea Pensioner. 'I'm sorry, Sir.' She respects the immaculate retired Army soldiers who live in the nearby Royal Chelsea Hospital. They're so well-dressed, in their tailored bright red coats and look fantastic on the fashionable King's Road.

Portia decides to have lunch before returning to her adorable house in Clover Mews - and Fabian. Deep down she knows it's a delaying tactic. She pushes the thought away. The sun is shining. It's a perfect day for people-watching and forgetting her cares. Oh, joy, there's an empty table outside Blossoms Cafe. She orders her favourite, chicken Kiev, with dauphinoise potatoes and a glass of the house white, and spends a pleasant hour watching the fashion parade.

The styles aren't as diverse as they'd been when she'd shopped with her mum in the 80's: Punks had their photos taken with Chelsea Pensioners, and new romantics strolled along, puffy sleeves billowing in the breeze. It was eclectic and electric with excitement. It's staider and more conventional now, but Portia can still feel the magic.

BACK HOME, PORTIA SHOUTS, 'Hello, Fabian, are you in?' No answer. She heads upstairs, to put her new twinset and tasselled loafers into the wardrobe.

She's horrified when she opens the bedroom door. A naked Fabian is bouncing up and down on top of someone, and a strong aroma of musky sweat, mingled with fruity aftershave fills the air. As Portia has always found her husband reluctant and timid in the passion department, she's shocked to see such frenetic action.

'What on earth is going on here?' she asks, aware of the cliché.

Fabian shrieks, leaps off his partner and runs into the bathroom.

Antoine, their handsome French chauffeur, is revealed in all his glory, wearing only his hat and a smug expression. 'We're in love!'

Portia storms downstairs into the kitchen and, hands shaking, pours a large brandy. She takes the drink into the living room and sits on one of two matching sofas, covered in a yellow floral fabric. She wants to chuck the brandy over them; the print was Fabian's choice; she'd wanted something less obviously feminine.

How has she not realised what was happening? Her husband's unexciting performance in bed, his stamp collection... Stamp collection? She marches over to where he hides the key and opens the cupboard to his prized possessions. The book labelled 'French Special Editions' is full of naked photos of Antoine. He looks excited in most of them. What a big boy! No wonder Fabian was keen to employ him.

Portia slams her antique crystal glass onto the table and goes to the bottom of the stairs. 'Get down here right now; we need to talk.'

Two minutes later a shamefaced Fabian and smug-faced Antoine appear in the living room. 'Not you, Antoine. You can get out now. And don't dare take the car. You can slum it on the tube. Get lost.'

Fabian has the good grace to say nothing. Antoine minces from the room. 'I'll be at home. Phone me later, darling.'

To her horror and disbelief, Fabian runs after him.

Portia bursts into tears.

Izzie Firecracker, May 1996

IZZIE FIRECRACKER GROANS, pulling off her red silk sleep mask, embroidered with the words *Wake Me for Coffee*. She drags herself up to rest against goose-down pillows. Has she survived the after-effects of three or four too many glasses of red wine in the Greedy Gourmet last night? She was celebrating another successful year of the Second Chance Club.

Yes, I do believe I have, she triumphs, thanks to the wonders of milk thistle, as recommended by the owner of the Worthy Nut health store, who swore it was incredible for taking the edge off hangovers. Water tonight, though. She knows if she has wine for a few days running it lowers her spirits and makes her look like crap. Now, there's a ditty she muses - *the higher the spirits, the lower the spirit.*

Dr Dhal, an ayurvedic practitioner, told her a glass of wine, or two, to enhance a good mood is fine - but use it, or any alcohol, to lift ill humour and it makes things worse. From experience, Izzie finds it true. But last night she was in a fabulous mood from start to finish and had a perfect time eye-flirting with the handsome man on the next table, who was dining with his mum; when she nipped to the loo, he asked for Izzie's phone number. She hopes he calls; she hasn't had a serious relationship for a few years but enjoys the occasional steamy romantic encounter.

Izzie needs coffee; she loves it, the taste and the smell, although Dr Dhal advised her to abstain. On his recommendation, she gave up the evil bean for a year but missed it dreadfully. Sitting in her favourite cafes with herbal teas felt sad, so her beloved java is back in her life, the real McCoy in the mornings, decaf after noon.

Some mornings she hops out of bed and throws on casual clothes, for the short walk to Brewed Awakening, where she enjoys a frothy cappuccino and an almond croissant. Today, Doris, her daily, places a perfect Americano on the bedside table: A far cry from when she would slam down a mug of Blandwell House instant. Izzie is her cleaner's heroine after helping transform her life from dreary to dazzling.

'Did anyone phone when I was sleeping, Doris? I was dead to the world.'

'Yes, love. You've had a message from a Portia Belmont-Flowers who wants you to call back. Oh, and I just remembered, the other lady I clean for wants an appointment, Martha her name is. She's fed up with her bully of a hubby. And I don't blame her.'

'You are a darling, Doris. I should pay you a commission.'

'Don't worry, love, I don't want it, and there's no need. I'd still be a drudge, at Benny's beck and call if it weren't for you. And anyhow, I don't need it now I've got my own cleaning company, Doris's Dailies. I have a team of ten, now.'

'Brilliant. Why do you still work as a cleaner yourself when you don't have to? You could put your feet up with a cup of tea and watch someone else slave away.'

'I love cleaning other people's houses but hate doing my own. One of the team does mine. I have the luxury of picking who I clean for and who works for me. And hubby does the books, as long as I keep him supplied with tea and biscuits. He likes chocolate digestives, along with a builder's brew.'

'Sounds perfect, Doris. You've come a long way.'

'I have. I looked and felt dreary and resented working for others all the time. I'd always wanted my own business, and my dream has come true. You rescued me, helped bring out my confident and fun side. But some people have no sense of humour, bless them. They don't understand I'm having a laugh when I call myself Doris Designer-Overall on my business cards.'

Doris's Dailies
Doris Designer-Overall
We cut the mustard, not the corners

'LOTS OF US NEED RESCUING sometimes, Doris. It was an angel called Anne who got me on the road to the Second Chance Club. I love my job, helping people get their lives back, or even appreciating what they have and are capable of, often for the first time.'

'Who's Anne?'

'It's a long story. I'll tell you one day. I wasn't always Izzie Firecracker. I was christened Isadora Hale, but changed my surname a few years ago, after the last divorce.'

'I'm not working tomorrow. How about we meet for lunch, my treat, and you can tell me your story. We can go to Da Vinci's if you want. I know you love their pizza.'

'It's a date, Doris,' says Izzie, thinking back.

Izzie, Liverpool 1960's

IZZIE, CHRISTENED Isadora, was living in London in the perfect apartment enjoying the ideal existence, it appeared. How could she dare admit to any unhappiness? If your life is like the characters in *Coronation Street* or you live in a leaky caravan, in somewhere like Scuddlethorpe or Grimlington it's acceptable to complain about being miserable. But live in a large flat in Knightsbridge, within strolling distance of Harrods, and dare admit you are not happy then sympathy may be in short supply.

Izzie's life didn't begin in such a salubrious setting. There was no silver spoon. For her first eight years, she lived in Liverpool, with her mum, dad and big brother in a terraced house, with no bathroom, and an outside lavatory. The next-door neighbours didn't even have an electric light in their toilet. One moonless night the boy next door burnt his bum on the candle he placed on the loo seat, and couldn't sit for over a week.

Izzie left Liverpool and moved 'over the water' to the Wirral in 1967 when she was eight, and her little brother was born. Her mum wanted a better life and an extra bedroom. Her dad, who worked as a tally clerk at Birkenhead docks, was sick of crossing the Mersey twice a day five days a week. And their house, along with the others on the street, was due for demolition.

They only moved a few miles away, but it could have been the moon. The Liverpool Izzie remembers from early childhood was buzzy and lively, due to the colourful and varied characters: There were so many.

MRS PAWLEY SHOWED NO sympathy for her kids when they hurt themselves. If they were almost bleeding to death from a fall, they'd get a slap, accompanied by a sympathetic cry of, 'You stupid bugger, gerrin the 'ouse!' But if someone else's little darlings sustained even the tiniest wound, she fussed over them like she was Florence Nightingale. The injured party was lead into her home, where she lovingly put a plaster over even the smallest cuts and grazes.

One day Izzie fell over, and this self-appointed nurse was the first to hear her cries. She rushed into the street, scooped Izzie up and carried her inside, applied TCP and put a plaster on the minuscule cut, saying, 'There-there my little lamb, it's all right there-there.' Before she took Izzie home, she gave her bourbon biscuits and cherry pop.

Izzie was confused. 'Mum, why was she so kind when I cut my knee but goes mad when her own children fall over?'

A cloud passed over her mother's face. 'It's to hide her fear; she's terrified when they have an accident. She wants to keep them safe.'

None of the parents complained if someone else took charge of their kids. It was an unwritten rule that everyone looked after everyone else, never more apparent than the day a dog called Sandy bit Izzie's arm. She'd tried to shake his paw, despite many angry growls of warning. Within seconds of her screams, almost the entire street population was out to help and offer sympathy.

MRS THREADGOLD SCRUBBED the pavement and steps outside her house most Mondays, rain or shine. She was in her eighties, with arthritic hands. Down on her knees, wearing a wrap-around floral pinafore over her clothes and with a metal bucket of water and container of Vim at her side, she scrubbed and scrubbed until her doorstep, and surrounding pavement turned from off-white to brilliant white.

After her labours, she stood guard wearing a grim expression of warning. As soon as anyone approached the hallowed ground, she warned, 'Gerroff me step!' Nobody dared walk over the sacred area and made safe detours onto the street, away from the scary expression on Mrs Threadgold's face and the pungent smell of bleach.

One sunny August day Izzie and her friend were pushing their prams along the road. A doll called Daffodil, who wore a red polka dot dress, was the beloved passenger in Izzie pram. Gillian's 'baby' was a teddy-bear, wearing pyjamas.

'Shall we dare push our prams over the white pavement Izzie?' asked her friend.

'No, Mrs Threadgold will go mad.'

'Cowardly cowardly custard, you can't eat mustard.'

'Oh, all right. It might be OK, we're only little.'

They advanced their prams like chariots going into battle.

'GERROFF ME STEP!'

They never tried it again.

MRS OGDEN ALWAYS WORE curlers with a hairnet over the top.

'What does she look like without them, Mum? Is her hair long or short?' Izzie asked.

'I wouldn't know. In ten years I've never seen her without them. I visited her house once, in July, and the Christmas decorations were still up. She told me it was to save putting them back up again on Christmas Eve.' Repelled by the odious idea, Izzie's mum, Rose, wrinkled her nose, patted her beautifully styled dark curls and smoothed her chic fitted blue dress.

Rose loved clothes and always looked smart, as did Izzie and her big brother.

'You'd think those kids were a pair of dolls, the way you dress them up,' grumbled Izzie's dad, Stan, with a proud expression.

ROSE WAS TREATING THE six-year-old Izzie to a new coat, and they were off into town to choose it. They were going to Cripps, on Bold Street, followed by Blackler's, Lewis's and George Henry Lee. In between stores, they were going to Henderson's cafe for refreshments.

At the bus stop, Izzie imagined the happy scenarios when a cheerful woman arrived with six small scruffy children in tow. Rose remarked on their beautiful skin. 'I'll tell you the secret,' said the proud mother, 'I wash their faces with a wet nappy.'

'Mum, you won't wash my face in baby wee if I ever have a little brother or sister, will you?' Izzie panicked once on the bus.

'No, Izzie. Let's stick with Camay.'

'Why were those children wearing plastic beach sandals in winter?'

'Not everyone can afford nice stout leather shoes like yours, Izzie. And you're a lucky girl to be getting a new coat.'

The shopping trip was a happy success. Izzie chose a green wool coat, trimmed with ivory faux fur collar and cuffs. When they were in Blackler's, she enjoyed a ride on the giant rocking horse, Blackie, a favourite of little children for miles around.

IN THE DAYTIME WHEN there was no school, and it didn't rain, most of the kids played outside, apart from short absences when the summons came for meal times or favourite TV shows.

Two favourite games were Relievo and Kick the Can, variations of Hide and Seek. There was a mass exodus indoors when a mum shouted something like 'Batman!' clearing the street in seconds. Everyone loved Batman but as soon as it finished the entire child population, over three years old, was out again, some of them wearing their mums' cardigans as superhero capes.

The big kids always kept an eye on the little ones, whether they wanted to or not.

When Izzie and family moved to their new house in Eastborough, she felt little of this atmosphere and group camaraderie, what she now knows to be a kind of magic, coherence, a coming together of group consciousness, merging the past and present.

The new housing estate hadn't developed its personality and lacked colour. People had experienced so much together, living in those Victorian terraced houses; there was a history. They'd lived through wars - and football matches.

Izzie remembers a day in 1966.

The girls were out playing with skipping ropes. Every so often they heard a roar - the street shook. There was electricity in the air. Then a group cry came from the houses culminating in one massive boom, not scary as it emanated triumph and joy.

Jubilant men poured into the street, handing money to Izzie and her mates, and then headed into the corner pub, singing.

It was time to celebrate: England had won the World Cup. Even though she'd been told not to take money from strangers, it was OK.

Everything was OK that day.

Izzie wanted that feeling back.

Ferry across the Mersey

CLIFF RICHARD SANG 'In the Country' from the taxi radio as Izzie, and her family moved to the Wirral countryside.

It was more like fields of mud, rather than country. They were moving to a new estate, courtesy of Mr Wimpey. Izzie misheard 'Mr Whippy', and hoped she was off to a land of endless ice-cream.

In those days, in the late 1960's, grassed gardens were rarely part of the deal with new homes; you often just got a path, and a pile of earth, front and back.

Moving day was a wet and cold day in January 1967 - lovely! There was mud everywhere, and Izzie's mum was fed up. All she did was alternate between mopping the floor and feeding the baby.

Izzie's new little brother was five weeks old, so she was now the middle child; at eight, sandwiched between her fourteen-year-old brother and the baby.

To add to the mood of joviality Izzie's grandmother, on her dad's side, came to 'help', which involved sloshing gallons of water onto already wet floors. Soon the new house resembled a pond. It wouldn't have surprised Izzie to see a frog on a lily pad at the edge of the living room.

Izzie's dad thought the world of his parents, which showed great loyalty, as they moved house when he was in the Navy, in

World War Two, without telling him. When he finally tracked them down, after VE day, it was to discover they'd spent the money he'd sent home to put in his savings account. Nice.

Izzie remembers her dad's parents as two of the most miserable people she's ever met. On Sundays, she was often dragged to visit their small dark flat in Birkenhead. It was gloomy and decorated with numerous religious images: statues and paintings.

Above the fireplace was a framed print of Jesus on the cross, with a bleeding head, from the crown of thorns and bloody hands and feet, from the nails. The image terrified young Izzie, but not as much as having to enter the bedroom:

One or other of the grandparents were usually ill. Most visits included sitting by their bed, next to a cabinet piled with pills and potions. One dark and gloomy day, her dad came out of the bedroom and said, 'Nan wants to see you, Izzie, go on in.'

'I don't want to go on my own. I'm scared.'

'Don't be silly; it's just an old woman in bed. What can happen to you? Do as I say.'

IZZIE PAUSED, TERRIFIED, outside the dingy door with yellowed paint. A dog howled in the distance. Plucking up courage she turned the knob and pushed; the door opened effortlessly but slammed shut once she was in the room.

A luminous green Jesus on the cross floated towards her.

She screamed.

'For goodness sake, Izzie,' scolded her dad. 'It's just a glow-in-the-dark ornament. Your nan sometimes likes the curtains closed when she's ill.'

The atmosphere of the flat was claustrophobic and depressing, and the air stuffy with a nauseatingly sweet smell and a thick feeling of doom. Izzie longed for fresh air and loved it when her cousins visited, and they were all allowed to play outside, where daylight soothed dark and childish fears, and her senses rejoiced in the smell of fresh air.

Agnes, Izzie's cousin, couldn't understand her fear of the religious images. 'I love the luminous Jesus on the cross; I've got one in my bedroom.' Izzie shuddered then forgot about it until she stayed with Agnes in the summer holidays, and they shared a room. On the first night, tired from the journey from the Wirral to Suffolk she collapsed into bed early, waking in the wee small hours to darkness, apart from the dreaded luminous green Jesus on the cross, hovering above her cousin's bed.

Izzie's screams woke everyone up. Agnes pursed her lips and put the wall ornament into a drawer. 'You *are* silly; it's lovely and makes me feel safe.'

The next day the sun shone, and the cousins ate ice-cream in the garden, listening to Scott McKenzie sing 'San Francisco' on the radio. All was right with the world. Agnes and Izzie gathered daisies and danced with flowers in their hair.

'Shall I put the ornament back on the wall, Izzie?'

'Don't you dare.'

A NEW HOUSE MEANT A new school. Izzie didn't realise she spoke with an accent until the kids made fun of her Liverpool one - not too much, those were the days of Beatlemania.

One lunchtime her classmates gathered around her, and a studious, handsome boy called Daniel. The other children thought they fancied each other and should get married. They put a plastic ring on Izzie's third finger left hand and made a circle around the happy couple, singing 'OB-LA-DI, OB-LA-DA...' at the tops of their voices. The eight-year-olds knew every word - the power of The Beatles.

The romance never came to anything apart from Daniel giving Izzie a cheese and onion crisp flavoured kiss, on a walk home from school when they were ten.

SCHOOL CARRIED ON WITH little incident. Izzie was, in the main, a happy child but sometimes tormented by a vivid imagination. Terrible things were often about to befall her, especially on dull days.

If the sun shone in the school holidays, she played outside, or if it was raining, she enjoyed lying on the sofa with a book. Amongst her favourites were the Jennings and Chalet School stories. She loved Noel Streatfield and visited London in her mind reading *Wintle's Wonders*. I'd like to live there one day, she thought, turning a page.

'Come on, Izzie, it's stopped raining, and the sun's out. Put your book away and let's go for a walk. We can go to the farm and buy some of those lovely sweet-smelling tomatoes for this evening's salad,' said her mum.

The tomatoes were so delicious and juicy they ate them like sweets on the sunny meander home: not one of them made it to the dinner table.

IN THE SUMMER HOLIDAYS of 1969, Izzie was waiting for The Letter which would tell her what school she'd attend in September. Had she passed the exams? What would her fate be - grammar school or the new secondary modern around the corner?

Unable to bear the suspense she cycled to the local library to take her mind off things. On the way back she saw Steve Mitchell, a classmate, on the side of the road, jumping up and down. 'I've passed! I've passed!'

Phew, thought Izzie; if he's passed, then I must have done.

Arriving home, she dashed through the front door. 'Has it come?'

A crestfallen Rose handed Izzie a letter. 'I'm sorry, you haven't passed. Look at the name of your new school.'

Without reading it, Izzie flung the offending piece of paper across the room. 'It's not fair. Steve Mitchell passed, and I'm cleverer than him.'

'Self-praise is no recommendation,' said Stan.

Rose picked up the letter and handed it to her daughter, 'I said, have a look at the name of your new school.'

Izzie read the name: Ashton's Grammar School for Girls. She'd passed.

But the moment was ruined.

Married to Tim, 1983

IZZIE WAS TWENTY-FOUR and had married the good-looking but tedious Tim in 1977. He was more than grating on her nerves; he was driving her nuts.

'Who've you been writing to?' he asked, arriving home from his work as an accountant one evening.

'What makes you think I was writing to anyone?'

'You've moved the pen that usually sits by the telephone.'

'Oh, for God's sake, you're like that detective, Kojak. Where's your lollipop? Are you ready for dinner?'

'Yes, but you haven't told me who you've been writing to.'

'I was writing a love letter to the electricity company to send along with the cheque.'

'There's no need to be sarcastic.'

'There's no reason to be anal retentive and dull either, but you make it your life's work.' Izzie left the room, closing the door as hard as she dared, screaming inside. She didn't risk making much noise lest he indulged in another of his long mopes, he could sulk for days.

Izzie moaned to her mate, Cindy, 'Oh God, what a dullard he is. What shall I do? I'm only twenty-four and have a husband who comes into the room when I'm in the bath, not to gaze at my naked form, but to check I'm not using too much hot water. The level shouldn't go above the imaginary line.'

'Imaginary line, what do you mean?' Cindy asked between guffaws.

'He took me by the hand into the bathroom and pointed out a level above which the water must not go.'

'What a tosser!'

'I'm daft to put up with it, but my wonderful husband doesn't do it to be nasty. These things worry him.'

TIM POPPED HIS NEAT head into the kitchen. 'You didn't plump up the cushions in the living room as I asked. And bits of last night's crisps are still on the carpet. I'm going into the garage to dry the car because it's wet from the rain. And don't put too many vegetables on my plate; you know I can't be over-whelmed with food. You gave me too many peas last night.'

IZZIE MET HER FUTURE first husband at a rugby club dance when she was sixteen and Tim twenty-two. She hadn't liked the idea because it would be an evening of soul music and she was more into rock bands. So was her best mate. However, Cindy's hormones were getting the better of her. 'Please come with me, Izzie. I don't want to go on my own, and this boy I fancy, Peter, has asked me along.'

'Chivalrous. Can't this knight in shining armour come and pick you up from home?'

Cindy sniggered. 'No, but I'd like to pick *him* up. He's part of the rugby team and has to be there to sort things out. Please come, we'll have something to eat and get ready at my house;

have a few sneaky drinks first. It'll be a laugh. I'll ask Mum to make her famous chocolate cake.'

'Oh, OK then, but you know we like flinging our heads about to Black Sabbath, rather than dance around our handbags to soul music.'

'We'll ask the DJ to play 'Paranoid', that'll be fun.' Cindy closed the deal.

They arrived late. There was a handsome, dark-haired man on the door, taking the entrance money. Izzie asked how much it was.

'Nothing,' he said. 'It wouldn't be fair; the dance is half over. I'll lock up the takings then I'm having a pint.'

The girls grinned; money to spend on their current favourite, lager and blackcurrant.

Cindy soon spotted her object of desire. 'There he is, Izzie. Come over and say hello.'

Peter didn't want Izzie cramping his style. After a perfunctory greeting, he said, 'Talk to my friend, Tim; he's over there.' He pointed to the man who'd refused the entrance money, now standing with a pint.

Izzie ambled towards her fate. After gazing into his intoxicating violet eyes, she was in lust within minutes, falling in love a few weeks later when he kissed her after eating strawberries, the delicious juice on his lips transferring to hers and tasting and smelling sublime.

She was a goner.

IZZIE AND CINDY WERE fourteen when they met at school, in a maths class. Izzie was sitting in the front row because she was too vain to wear her hideous glasses. An optician had diagnosed her short-sighted a few months earlier, much to her horror.

'But I don't want to wear glasses, Mum. I hate them already.'

'Don't be silly, Izzie.'

It wasn't even as if there were boys in her school: They were incarcerated next door, in an identical, but grimier, building.

Miss Fells, the maths teacher, was droning on about the hair on a hippopotamus or something when Izzie had an impulse to look towards the back of the classroom: Anywhere other than Miss Fell's disapproving, stern face or the hieroglyphics on the blackboard. She had little desire to turn to page 33 of her textbook.

Having performed a nearly 180-degree turn of the head, Miss Fells would've been impressed at the terminology, the morning lesson before break livened up.

Sitting two rows behind was a girl in a green uniform, everyone else's was blue. She wore a bored expression and conspirator's grin, directed straight at Izzie. They knew they'd be friends. For the next fifteen minutes, even though Miss Fells was as boring as ever, judging by the numerous yawns distributed amongst the thirty girls, maths was less dull.

They got together at morning break and introduced themselves. Cindy was in a green uniform because it was her first day at the school and her mum hadn't got round to getting her the regulation one, making her wait until her dad's next pay cheque.

'The cow!' said Cindy, biting into a Cadbury's Creme Egg. 'Why don't you come over after school tomorrow? Mum makes a great chocolate cake.'

Izzie was excited. 'It sounds great, thanks. I'll check with Mum, but I'm sure it'll be OK.'

With all this talk of chocolate products, you might think they were plus-size girls who had found their soul mates or eating buddies. But they were a 'pair of string beans', to quote a teacher. They planned their entire school day around food, not lessons. They usually got seconds at lunchtime, snacked during breaks, and surreptitiously, they hoped, ate sweets during lessons.

In history, Mr Wiggins wanted to know which girl was taking off her nail varnish because he could smell acetone, but it was pear drops.

'Do you want one, Mr Wiggins?' Izzie asked. She got away with it, as usual. They got away with most things. Maybe because they were cute, or at least people told them they were: Cindy's caramel-coloured hair was just above shoulder length, and wild, *a floor mop*, her dad called it.

Izzie's was long, nut-brown and straight with a slight kink. *Rats' tails*, her dad called it.

'That's not nice, Stanley,' said Izzie's mum.

Stan chuckled.

THE PROMISED CHOCOLATE cake was fantastic. To this day it's the best Izzie has tasted. And it had Smarties on top of the gooey icing - bliss. Izzie kept complimenting Cindy's mum on it, hoping for a third slice, which didn't materialise.

Cindy's dad was eccentric. 'What does your father do, Izzie?'

She was surprised at the mundane question from such an unconventional person. When she swivelled to answer, he had a cheese straw up each nostril, and said, 'I hear you have a new teacher in your school, Master Bates, is that right?'

Izzie spat out a mouthful of dandelion and burdock.

'What do you want to be when you grow up, Izzie?' said Cindy

'Don't know yet.'

I want to be a nurse, don't I, Mum?'

'Yes, Cindy, when other little girls were putting pretty dresses on their dolls, you were wrapping yours in bandages, and listening to their hearts with a toy stethoscope.'

Cindy's arrival was a godsend. Since Izzie's family had left Liverpool, she'd turned down the volume on her personality.

No more. Life was fun. Instead of attending tea parties, with Donny Osmond adoring classmates, off she and Cindy gallivanted to rock concerts. They wore jeans with massive flares, called loons, and scoop-neck t-shirts. Cindy circled her eyes with bright blue eye shadow, Izzie opted for green. They flung masses of love beads around their necks and doused themselves in patchouli oil. 'It smells like cat's pee,' said Cindy's mum, crinkling her nose.

Black Sabbath, Hawkwind, Nazareth - life was fun. One night when they were at the Liverpool Guild of Students, pretending to be undergraduates at the university, they got to see a new band, Queen, for thirty-five pence. They could only stay for half an hour, lest they missed the last ferry across the Mersey.

They ran all the way to the Pier Head, and poor Cindy fell off her red wooden platform clogs, ripping her favourite jeans and cutting her knees. Where was Mrs Pawley, with plasters, TCP and kind words?

'What time is the last ship?' a toothless crone asked as they arrived at the Pier Head, eliminating the last vestige of glamour from the evening.

THE FRIENDS EXPERIENCED many adventures until Izzie got engaged to Tim, whose good looks lured her into a less colourful world. With his violet eyes and a double row of black lashes, he looked as if he'd be at home on a Harley, riding without a helmet, the wind in his hair.

Instead, Tim was the proud owner of a dull brown Austin Allegro, with an almost square steering wheel - to match his personality. He never left the car, even for two minutes, without putting on the crook lock; a clumsy security device which immobilised the steering wheel to stop any passing opportunistic thieves from driving the car away.

'What idiot would nick that awful thing?' his mates teased. 'You'd be better off putting a sign on the window saying, please drive me away.'

And Tim loved and depended on his lists, labelled 'Long Term List' and 'Short Term List'. His long-term list included such easy-to-forget tasks such as 'paint the house'. The short-term included mind joggers like 'buy bread'.

'How could you forget to paint the house if it's not written on a list?' Izzie asked.

'That's not the point. Lists make me feel secure. And are we low on beans? If so I'll put them on my short-term list.'

Tim always made sure the tins in the cupboard faced forward in neat rows. He went into a panic if baked bean supplies ran low, as he loved them. One day he asked Izzie why there was a tin of beans in the larder with a 25p label on when they were only 19p in SaveFast.

Years later, when Izzie saw the cupboard scene in *Sleeping with the Enemy*, she was taken right back, however, unlike the abusive Martin Burney, Tim was never violent; apart from his epic sulks he was a pussycat.

The front door was for visitors only. When they weren't 'entertaining', a misnomer if ever there was one, they used the back door to enter and exit the house: Tim's orders, as he worried the hall carpet would get dirty.

Izzie had made the fatal mistake of being seduced by his looks, and there she was, in her prime, living a life most eighty-year-olds would find dull. It might be livelier to live in the local nursing home, Bygones.

'It's chilly in here,' she said as they 'relaxed' in the living room one evening, watching *One Flew over the Cuckoo's Nest*.

'Go outdoors and come back in again, so you'll feel the benefit,' said Tim, 'I'll stop the video. There's no need to waste money turning up the gas fire.'

'Don't be ridiculous, turn the flipping heat up; even Nurse Ratched wouldn't be that mean.'

The metaphorical last straw snapped one evening when Izzie announced, 'I'm nipping to see Mum and Dad before supper.' Her parents lived four miles away.

'Go on your bike,' said Tim. 'The weather forecast says rain and I don't want the car to get wet and have to spend ages wiping it down.'

You'd think it was some rare classic, a vintage Rolls Royce or something, not the Allegro. And what a cheek he wasn't worried about his wife getting wet. 'I'm going in the sodding car,' said Izzie, knowing she'd have to endure another of his long sulks.

She'd had enough. Marriage to Tim was depressing. She gave out a bright exterior but was dying inside.

IZZIE VISITED HER DOCTOR and told him she felt sad, anxious and dreaded the future. The thought of life with Tim going on and on, leading ahead on an endless road, with no happy surprises was horrific. She could be dramatic, but this was no exaggeration. She had a problem getting through each day and escaped to bed earlier and earlier to block everything out.

She got on well with her GP and had been visiting him alone since she was ten. Her mum's humble attitude, typical of many of her generation, had often embarrassed Izzie. To Rose, and others, a doctor was like royalty, a deity, or both; rolled into one imposing presence.

Doctor Jackson put down his pen. 'I'm going to stick my neck out here. I've always thought you such a happy patient, bounding in here with a smile, even when you came on your own with terrible tonsillitis. I was concerned when I found out who you married. Tim used to be one of my patients, so I know what he's like; a nice person but too gloomy for you. I thought he might drag you down and he has. Maybe you should go your separate ways, for your health and sanity.'

Izzie knew the doctor was right and was relieved he didn't think her depression and anxiety was serious, or she was going mad.

Do you know the feeling when you marry the man of your dreams, and you expect everything to be perfect? And it isn't; it's downhill after the excitement of the wedding day. You keep on and on, thinking when this happens, and that happens you'll reach Nirvana. 'Nirvana' never arrives, and you sink deeper into hell.

Izzie realised her potential mistake the day after their wedding. There she was, set for a languorous, romantic morning in the honeymoon suite when Tim said, 'Hurry and drink your coffee; we've got to get home. I've arranged for a mate to plumb in the washing machine.'

THE HONEYMOON IN BENIDORM was a nightmare. Tim spent most of the fortnight sulking or getting jealous every time another man noticed her. Or, much worse, spoke to her. One day that started well ended badly because a swarthy and striking man asked Izzie the time, in all innocence. Tim thought he must have an ulterior motive, hadn't forgotten his watch and planned to lure her away. She wished.

'If it was innocent, why didn't he ask me what the time was?' asked Tim. 'It's obvious he was using it as an excuse to talk to you. I bet you fancy him, too, he's good looking.'

'Oh, for God's sake, you're driving me nuts, Tim!'

On another day he stomped back to the hotel to sulk when Izzie bought a bottle of cola from a beach stall. Tim thought the price was extortionate and accused her of being irresponsible and squandering money.

'Are you insane, Tim? It's a bottle of pop; I haven't splashed out on a Spanish villa!'

'That's not the point; you bought from the first stall and should have compared prices. You want to throw money away.'

BACK FROM THE HONEYMOON, Izzie dropped Tim at the office and drove the Allegro quite fast towards work - she was late. Overtaking, she lost control of the car due to the silly square steering wheel, and it bounced off the side of a lorry. As there were no angry beeps or two-finger salutes she kept on driving, with clammy hands and palpitating heart. Oh no, Tim's pride and joy! But there was probably just a little graze. At the car park, she nervously inspected the damage. Oh, shit - a significant dent in the passenger door.

She phoned Tim, thinking he'd be relieved she was OK. 'Oh, no, Izzie. That's all I need. How bad is the damage? How could you be so careless?'

No, married life was not the Utopia Izzie had imagined, far from it. But she was not quite ready to accept defeat; those striking eyes were hard to resist.

Nice secure job in the bank

IZZIE WAS SIXTEEN, and desperate for money. She hated her glasses and wanted contact lenses, but they cost eighty pounds. 'Mum, I hate my glasses, can I have contact lenses?'

'Yes, Izzie, of course, you can, if you pay for them. There's nothing wrong with your glasses, and you look nice in them.'

Nice? Bah! She resembled Colonel Blink, the Short-Sighted Gink, from *the Beezer*. Most of the time she managed without glasses, but it was tricky only seeing faces as distant blurs when she was out and about. If she wasn't sure if it was a stranger or someone known approaching she gave a half wave, half scratch of the head to cover all bases. She didn't want to offend a person by ignoring them.

It wasn't only lenses Izzie wanted; it was half of Chelsea Girl. She decided not to go back to school after 'O' levels. So, instead of joining the sixth form, in the September, she went for a few interviews and accepted a post at the local National Bank.

THE JOB WAS A NOVELTY, to begin with, and only a ten-minute walk or a five-minute run from home, which meant extra time for sleep. Perfect. It was much better than school when she'd had to be at the bus stop by 7.50 am. She loved her bed.

At first, she was in the machine room, keying transactions into a giant computer, printing cheque books and filing endless paperwork, which got monotonous. The boredom sometimes lead to mistakes. One day a customer queried an entry on her statement: 'I don't understand what this debit, labelled 'By P Honk' means. I don't know anyone called P Honk.'

Izzie went through the paper receipts for the day in question and laughed when she spotted the error. She'd misread a poorly written 'By Phone' and typed it into the computer incorrectly.

'It was a computer glitch, Madam. Please accept our apologies.'

After six months of slaving in the machine room, the bank promoted her to a grade two clerk, which included cashiering. Izzie loved being on the counter, chatting with the customers. She liked the cheerful school dinner ladies, who came with their pay cheques from the council every Wednesday.

'Hello, Izzie love. I know I'm supposed to wait for this cheque to clear, but can you cash it today? I've seen a lovely dress I want for my daughter's wedding, but I'm worried it'll sell before I've got the money.'

'I'm not supposed to, Mrs Pearson. But, OK, I don't suppose a cheque from the council will bounce but don't tell anyone.'

'Mum's the word, love. Thanks.'

Mrs Pearson must have announced Izzie's relaxed manner with a megaphone: The next Wednesday there was a queue of dinner ladies at her till that almost snaked out of the front door.

On tea break, a workmate said, 'You'd better watch it, Izzie, you could get into trouble with Mr Grove. My mum's a dinner lady. One of her mates said that if she wants her wages immediately to go to your counter because you'll cash a bus ticket.'

Mr Grove was the manager, and Izzie liked him. She flicked back her long hair. 'I'm sure the manager knows; he's not daft. He pulled me to one side the other day and said he's noticed the long queue at my counter on Wednesdays, and winked.'

The manager called Izzie into his office. 'My wife and I were chatting last night. She likes to come to your till when she pops in because she finds you cheerful. Last night she said you should have a more exciting job and I agree. I don't want to get rid of you, but working here is dull for someone as lively as you. But, while you *are* here, try and tone it down, you're too friendly and chatty with customers. Also, some of the clothes you wear are inappropriate, like the sweatshirt you're wearing today with IDONTGOTO UNIVERSITY on the front. You're not working behind a bar.'

Izzie didn't know whether to feel flattered or deflated. Maybe she should look for another job? Her colleagues were friendly, apart from the detestable Mr Swindell, the sub-manager: He had a nasty manner, and she didn't trust him.

The bank had a large trolley, used for pushing notes and heavy bags of coins in and out of the safe. Most people were careful of it, wary of hurting anyone. One day, Izzie was sure Mr Swindell aimed the vehicle at her. He ran it over her foot, shouting, 'Get out of my way!'

What a charmer, Izzie thought, bathing a nasty bruise that evening - he was making life a misery.

The day after the trolley incident she complained to Mr Grove. 'Don't tell tales, sort it out yourself,' he said. Then he looked remorseful and surprised Izzie by saying, 'I can't handle him either; he scares me with that terrible temper.'

'Thanks for telling me, Mr Grove. It makes me feel better.' And it did. What a lovely man.

HELLINGLY MENTAL HOSPITAL was near the bank. Some patients were allowed out alone on Wednesdays. One of these was Mr Halfpenny, who appeared at Izzie's till requesting a transfer of one million pounds from his current to savings account. She couldn't find a record of him so popped to see the manager. 'Send him in,' he said, finger touching the side of his nose.

Ten minutes later Mr Halfpenny emerged from the office with a satisfied smile, shook Mr Grove's hand and strutted through the front door.

'What the heck was all that about?' Izzie asked the head cashier.

'The poor man lost all his money in the stock market a few years back and went mad. He still thinks he's stinking rich, and often asks to transfer large amounts from one account to another. The manager humours him. Mr Halfpenny hasn't even got an account here.'

'Is that his real name?'

'Yes, maybe he should change it to Mr Coffers, Mr Gold, or something.'

MR SWINDELL CONTINUED to wear Izzie down. Thinking about finding a new job, she dawdled to work one day, after a doctor's appointment.

Sitting at the typewriter was a glamorous young woman, with chic short blonde hair. Her eyes were wet with tears. Izzie liked her on sight. 'Hello, I'm Izzie, what's the matter?'

'I'm Ginny. I hate bloody typing. They never made me type in my last job, at the Middling bank.'

'Don't worry; I'm sure you're only doing it because it's the usual typist's day off. You'll probably be cashiering tomorrow. Hey, let's go on the same lunch-break later.'

'Great, thanks. I'm glad I've met someone friendly on my first day.'

At lunch, they escaped to the local pub. Izzie found Ginny even more glamorous when she found out she was married. 'It must be fun with no parents to boss you about; I'd like to marry Tim. I will if he asks me.'

Ginny sprayed herself with Rainier of the Ritz, a sensual woody-floral fragrance, before reapplying a tawny lipstick. 'Don't get married until you're at least twenty-five. My wedding was last year. I'm only twenty-one. Come on; we'd better get back. I can't be late on my first day.'

Ginny cashiered next to Izzie the following morning. They had a ball, laughing and joking with the customers, and planned the same lunchtime again.

A man with a large bag of coins to pay in headed towards Izzie as she prepared to escape. She pretended not to see him, and dropped her pen on the floor, bending to pick it up. Izzie held her breath, phew, he moved to another cashier.

'You naughty girl,' scolded Ginny, as they headed out the door.

'I know, but I didn't want to miss our lunch together. Let's get chips and eat them in the park.'

Izzie didn't heed Ginny's advice about waiting until she was twenty-five to get married, and manacled herself to Tim when she was nineteen. She should have listened to her wise friend.

IZZIE WAS RELIEVED when Ginny voiced her feelings about the sub-manager. They both hated him covering when they skipped off to lunch. If a cashier station didn't balance and nobody could account for the discrepancy all staff that'd stood in signed for the difference in funds. Mr Swindell always refused, saying he never made mistakes. The toad!

The others let him get away with it, but Ginny and Izzie argued, which annoyed him, and he punished them with crappy jobs, such as toiling in the machine room, filing, typing or counting endless bags of coins.

'Don't dawdle counting those pennies, Izzie. I'm timing you.'

'I want those letters finished before you go home, Ginny.'

They hated him. 'I wish I hadn't said I could type, on my blinking application form,' said Ginny.

They got their own back. Everyone, except the manager, sub-manager, and branch-accountant took it in turns to make teas and coffees when the bank closed at 3.30. When it was Izzie's or Ginny's turn, they dunked a rancid, smelly dish-mop in Mr Swindell's beverage.

'Why are you watching me drink my tea? Get on with your work,' said the sub-manager, taking an appreciative sip. 'Ah, that's delicious.'

ONE DAY MR SWINDELL reached his pinnacle of horridness.

It was Izzie's job to post the letters and statements. She lived the closest to the bank, and the others were in a rush to get home. The last local pick up time was 5 pm. Mr Swindell delighted in making her wait until the last minute before she could dash to the post office. 'Don't you dare take the mail until my last letter is ready, Izzie,' he would taunt, even if there was lots of other post waiting to go.

He always took an age with his final missive of the day, signing it, sealing the envelope and putting on a stamp in triple slow motion. One day Izzie could tell from his sneering, and smug expression that he'd left it too late on purpose. It was five minutes past five before he finished the final letter. 'I've missed the deadline, Mr Swindell. The last post isn't until 6 pm in Beblington on your route home. Will you post them, please?'

He dripped with disdain. 'No, I can't, I'm in a hurry, and I'm not doing your job for you. You can get the bus and woe betide you if the letters arrive late.'

He got his comeuppance.

THE POLICE ARRESTED him. Head Office had been investigating for ages and had conclusive evidence he'd fiddled the bank out of masses of money. Izzie was a little sorry for him until she found out one of his victims was a sweet old lady, Mrs Minch, who he'd been 'advising' on investments; *give all your money to me, dear.*

He'd also embezzled substantial funds from a prominent local company, Land and Sea Engineering.

As a testament to his charm, Mr Grove persuaded the old lady and the company to stay with the bank.

After the police hauled Mr Swindell away in handcuffs, everyone was agog for details, and the staff room buzzed.

'I wonder what he was spending it on.' Izzie mused. 'Not clothes, judging by the scruffy creased suits and dingy shirts. And he often smelled of damp and mildew.'

Ginny looked thoughtful. 'Hmmm, maybe he had a floozy, and his clothes emitted a damp aroma because he had to wash his socks, shirt and underpants in a hotel sink, after their dirty and dangerous liaisons.'

Izzie grimaced. 'Eww – yuck!'

Perhaps the floozy theory wasn't far from the truth: The branch accountant did some amateur sleuthing and found out Mr Swindell's wife was unaware of extra money in the family coffers.

LIFE MOVED ON WHEN a pleasant, but dull, new sub-manager, Mr Dillard arrived, and speculation about Mr Swindell faded into the past where it belonged.

Mr Dillard moaned at Ginny and Izzie for wearing make-up. 'My wife doesn't need it. She's beautiful without all that artifice. She's having a Plasticware party later this week, come along.'

The Plasticware challenge was hard to resist. Izzie and Ginny wanted to see this vision of natural loveliness for themselves. They checked Mr Dillard wouldn't be at home; 'I'll be out on Thursday. It's my pottery class,' he assured them. Thank God! They saw more than enough of him at work.

Arriving at the Dillard residence, Ginny knocked on the door. A plump woman with long greasy hair, spotty pale face, and smelling of stale sweat opened it. 'Come in,' she said. 'I'm Jenny Dillard.'

Izzie and Ginny hardly dared glance at each other for the entire evening, lest they exploded with suppressed giggles.

The next day Mr Dillard was eager to know what they thought of his makeup-free wife. 'You're right,' said Ginny. 'But she's lucky; Izzie and I couldn't get away with the natural look.'

Mr Dillard looked proud and asked what they'd bought at the party.

'*Stash and Dash* containers to keep cosmetics in,' said Izzie.

'Are you OK? The two of you are red in the face.' Mr Dillard scratched his head in confusion as they both ran towards the Ladies', hands over their mouths.

GINNY TOLD IZZIE SHE was pregnant and would leave in a few months. That was it. Izzie must find another job; the bank would be too staid without her fun partner in crime. After a few weeks of desperate searching, she applied for a post as a beauty consultant. When she got the acceptance letter, she was ecstatic. She would start the new job before Ginny's maternity leave began, which was disappointing.

'Perhaps Jenny Dillard can be one of your first customers,' said Ginny, with a wink.

The staff had a whip-round to buy a farewell present, nominating Ginny to choose it, and she asked Izzie what she wanted. That was an easy question to answer - a perfect maxi-dress she'd seen in Lewis's of Liverpool. It was royal blue with a star cut-out at the bust, covered in net.

'You'd better act surprised when you open it,' warned Ginny. 'I'm supposed to keep the gift a secret.'

On Izzie's final day, after the bank closed its doors at 3.30, Mr Grove presented her with a card, a bunch of flowers and a gift wrapped in elegant silver paper, tied with a big blue bow. She opened it there and then. 'Oh, this is a lovely surprise. What a fabulous dress, it's divine. I can't wait to wear it. Thank you so much, I love it.'

'That was rubbish,' Ginny told her later. 'You overacted so much it was obvious you knew what you were getting.'

'Sorry, Ginny, but thanks so much for organising it all.'

Izzie loved her gift and modelled it that evening when her parents came over to visit.

Tim looked angry. 'I don't know where you'll wear it. That's not a suitable garment for a married woman; you look like you're on the pull. And you should have asked for the standard lamp we want, not some stupid dress.'

Rose shook her head in annoyance. 'She's twenty, not fifty, and looks lovely in it. But I still don't understand why you left your nice secure job at the bank, Izzie. You could have stayed until you retired.'

'There's your answer, Mum.'

Izzie sells makeup

AT FIRST, WORKING ON the Chantelle counter in Greens of Chester was glamorous, after the bank. But after a few years, Izzie was becoming bored again, and it didn't help having to go home to Tim every evening. Her life was colourless for one so young.

Many of the customers were nice, but she was tired of the ones who thought their existence was dependent on finding the exact shade of lipstick or foundation. Izzie loved clothes and makeup but believed they should be fun, not taken seriously: Although, her mum made her laugh when she recalled Izzie refusing to leave the house without gloves, hat and handbag when she was three.

There was a customer so obsessed with finding the Holy Grail of the foundation world that she phoned the department at least once a week, sometimes every day, asking for a different counter or consultant from time to time. For the last few weeks, it had been Izzie's turn: 'Mrs Foundation wants you on the phone,' the Elizabeth Harding consultant called.

'Don't shout,' boomed the floor manager, in a louder voice.

Izzie picked up the phone with dread, adopting a cheerful tone. 'Hello Mrs Foun', erm, Mrs Jones. What can I do for you today?'

'The last foundation you sold me, Sulphur Glow, makes me look rather yellow. Which shade would you suggest and can you post it out today?'

Izzie wanted to suggest she got a life, realising she was one to talk; this could be her soon. She now knows that when we're not happy inside, we focus more and more on outer trivia to avoid inner demons.

Izzie liked the women at work, apart from a few she wasn't too enamoured with, who could be bitchy.

Poppy worked part-time at the perfume counter to help pay for college. She had copper Pre-Raphaelite hair and the face of an angel, like a painting by Rossetti. Izzie has never, to this day, seen anyone so lovely: Stunning without a scrap of makeup, and a sweet soul. One weekend Poppy was strolling along a pavement when a car careered off the road and killed her.

Her ethereal beauty had created jealousy in the department and after she died a handful of staff had little sympathy.

Izzie felt terrible guilt; she'd arranged to meet Poppy for coffee the day she died but cancelled at the last minute. If she'd gone might her presence have stopped Poppy being on the pavement at the crucial moment? Or would they both have been killed?

THE FUNERAL WAS HEARTBREAKING, and when Poppy's boyfriend brought her little Yorkshire terrier, Hilton, into the church, the mourners wept.

'What on earth's the matter with you, Izzie?' asked one of the bitches.

'I'm upset after Poppy's funeral.'

'Don't be stupid, you hardly knew her. You only wanted an excuse for time away from work.'

Izzie tried to stay away from the unpleasant women as much as possible and put her attention on the fun and quirky ones. She'd always loved eccentrics. Her favourite was Cordelia, in her fifties, attractive but with an eye that looked soupy and unfocused. She spoke with a posh accent, and Izzie got the impression she was from a wealthy family.

During a break, the girls were discussing their favourite TV show, *Dallas*. Hardly anyone missed it, Tuesday evenings were sacred. It was Tim's night for rugby training, and Izzie revelled in time alone, watching the goings on at Southfork, and tucking into a baked potato with cheese. Pamela Ewing was beautiful, and the women in the department loved to copy her hair and makeup.

Cordelia asked, 'What's *Dallas*? I retired to bed with a Daphne du Maurier and had a glorious evening. I'm thinking of redoing my living room to resemble a beach, with deckchairs and sand. What do you say?'

She got a frosty reception from most, but Izzie thought it was cute and funny: 'Oh Cordelia that sounds fabulous. I will come round with ice-cream. Will you charge me rent for the deck chair?'

Izzie was about to take her driving test and asked Cordelia why she'd never learned to drive. 'I'm blind in one eye.'

'How on earth did that happen, Cordelia?' asked Izzie, hoping she wouldn't upset her.

'A one-armed man ran over me in his car, when I was four.'

ANOTHER FAVOURITE SUBJECT for the girls, at break time, apart from *Dallas*, was Izzie's marriage to Tim. They found it hysterical and often asked for the latest instalment. Cherie, an amateur actress, wanted to co-write a play called *Life with Tim*, or maybe *Bean There*. Cherie would play the role of Izzie. 'Has he said anything else that'd be perfect for our production?'

'He told me off this morning for not leaving my slippers together when I took them off, said they made the kitchen look untidy.'

Cherie frowns. 'What do you mean?'

'I didn't neatly put them side by side; they were at an untidy angle to each other. He wanted me to straighten them.'

'And did you?'

'No, I told him to bugger off.'

'I love it. Come on, one more thing, Izzie. There must be something; I haven't seen you for a few days.'

'I also got into trouble for eating one of the Breakout biscuits he keeps in stock for his packed lunches. He'd rationed them out in his mind to last the week, and me eating one upset the applecart, or should I say the biscuit barrel.'

Cherie was banging the table, tears of mirth rolling down her face.

Izzie decided to be ruthless. 'Last time we had sex he didn't even take his pyjama bottoms off, he lazily poked Mr Perky through the front fly.'

Cherie fell off the chair, holding her stomach.

Izzie didn't want to try harder to make her marriage work. She wanted out. Poor beautiful Poppy's life had been snuffed out almost before it had begun and Izzie didn't want to waste hers.

THAT EVENING AS TIM ate beans on toast, only one round of bread lest he was overwhelmed, she dropped a bomb. 'This isn't working, we should get divorced.'

Tim looked pensive, as he chewed and swallowed a mouthful of the gourmet feast. 'That's a good idea, I've known for ages I'm not right for you, too dull. You should live it up, somewhere like London, whereas I'm content to potter in the shed or play rugby. I've been wondering about it for a while. I'll be glad to have the pressure off.'

Cheek! Why was he not in floods of tears, begging her to stay? It was that simple. Well, not quite. What had she done?

The next day she panicked and wanted back into her fake comfort zone. She tried to change her mind, but too late - Tim was adamant - he phoned the estate agents to sell the house and packed to move back in with his parents, leaving her the car, planning on borrowing his dad's for a while. One of Tim's mates came to pick him up, and away they drove.

Izzie was devastated.

For two days. On the third day, driving to work, the sun came out, and Dire Straits belted out 'Romeo and Juliet' from the radio - ironic. All was right with the world. She experienced a tremendous whoosh of joy and an enormous sense of freedom. She'd escaped from a dark prison into a sunny land filled with endless possibilities. And inspiration struck, Tim was right, she shouldn't stay here.

She was off to London.

Breaking points, May 1996

JAMES PATS HIS TUMMY. 'I want another helping of spotted dick, with more custard this time.'

'What's the magic word?' Martha knows she sounds like a nanny, but is sick of the rudeness.

'Please, dearest. I hope I don't have to stand on ceremony when we have our weekly rumpy-pumpy later; you should be gagging for it.'

Martha knows who she'd like to gag. 'And why is that?'

'Well, nothing should have changed since our weekend in Paris, you were keen then, and I'm still a fine figure of a man. I haven't let myself go like you have.'

'No, James, you're perfect.' Paris was over twenty years ago! He's twice the figure he was. She must check the mirror in his dressing room; maybe he's sneaked in one of the fairground ones that make people look tall and skinny.

Martha dollops more spotted dick into his bowl. At least she's the same weight as when she walked up the aisle to her doom. What she's 'let go' is most of her confidence and happiness. She knows she looks careworn and tired, but the awful clothes James chooses add at least ten years to her appearance. She pours custard liberally over the sponge, wanting to pour it over his head, and then bangs the bowl down on the table.

Without a thank you, he picks up the spoon and shovels spotted dick into his mouth, like a pot-bellied pig at a trough.

Doris had a go at her today, said she's a doormat, and James has always been a control freak, wanting everyone under his thumb and no one to outshine him. It's a terrible thought, but Martha wonders if the reason James won't acknowledge their son's problems is that it suits him to have Simon below par. If the lad is busy being debauched; drinking, socialising and recovering from hangovers he's less likely to outperform Dad in business or any walk of life. Simon brought home impressive school reports over the years, but James never appeared pleased, and, God forbid, seemed jealous.

When Simon told them he didn't want to go to university Martha could have sworn James's mouth formed a satisfied smirk.

At the altar, she experienced a frisson of apprehension, after seeing her fiancé's mask slip, but put it down to wedding nerves. Also, she didn't find him exciting in bed, and nothing like her favourite heroes in books and movies but hoped matters would improve after marriage. They didn't. Their sex life was, and is, robotic, emotionless and lacking in passion. His erotic foreplay line is, 'How about it Martha? I need to relieve my stress.'

Her life has turned out like a fairytale - grim! The thought of the weekly 'rumpy-pumpy' makes her nauseous. James writes the appointments in the diary, with the code RP. A headache is in order. Otherwise, she might kill him. What should she use as a weapon? A rolling pin, maybe, or perhaps bash him over the head with a frozen chicken, then destroy the evidence by making coq au vin.

She saw something similar in an *Alfred Hitchcock Presents* episode when Mary, played by Barbara Bel Geddes, of Miss Ellie fame, killed her husband with a frozen leg of lamb, then roasted it and fed it to the investigating officers. Maybe she should watch it again, get some tips.

Shaking her head to remove the terrible thoughts, she resolves to phone Izzie Firecracker the next day. Martha wants a better life; not one spent rotting in prison.

James gets up from the table, emitting a loud garlic and custard infused belch. 'I'm off to bed to read the property section. I'll leave you to put the dishes in the washer. See you upstairs. I have some stress to relieve.' He gives a lascivious wink.

Martha feels sick.

WOLF SONG LAZES FULL length on the sofa, which he's pulled to within three feet of the TV, as he enjoys *Top of the Pops*, full blast. The room reeks of stale air and salt and vinegar crisps. He's been watching telly all day, with the window closed.

Carlotta sits on her chair in its usual place, under the window. She wants to watch *Friends*, which is on soon. Wolf is blocking the view. The entire situation is unreasonable, yet she knows if she says anything he will turn things around to make it her fault. She hasn't dared try recently but tonight gives it a go, as an experiment. Knowing she will see Izzie Firecracker soon has bolstered her confidence:

'Wolf.'

Nothing.

'WOLF!'

Wolf turns down the deafening volume. 'Ouch! I cricked my neck; you should have come over here. And there was no need to shout; you could have damaged my sensitive eardrums. You should have respect for other people.'

'Perhaps you should, too, Mr Colin Cooper.'

'My name is Wolf Song: you're disrespecting me again. I call *you* by your proper name.'

'I haven't just changed it to something silly, like 'erm Moon Beam.'

'My new name is *not* silly; it shows my evolved spirituality, you're not such an advanced soul as I, that's why you're not ready for an original name. You feel a need to fit in with others, like a sheep.'

'No, I'm not as advanced as you, Wolf. Anyway, I want to watch *Friends* after this has finished.'

'But there's a football match on; my team is playing. I've followed Knockimdown Rovers all my life. How can you ask me to miss something so important for a silly show where people sit around not doing anything apart from drink coffee?'

Hello, earth to Colin Cooper.

'Enjoy the match, Wolf, watching men run around a field after a ball might suit your evolved spirituality. I'm going next door for a glass of wine with Nerys.'

'What did you say?'

'Nothing, Wolf. See you later.'

Looking petulant, Wolf turns up the volume and returns to a supine position.

Make it a bottle of wine. Carlotta closes the front door before heading down the path.

PORTIA IS HAVING DINNER with her mum in the Leddington, Notting Hill, and has told her all about Fabian being gay. They are enjoying roast scallops and asparagus, with a crisp Chenin Blanc.

Her mum reaches over the table and takes Portia's hand, kind eyes sympathetic. 'Darling, I never thought Fabian was right for you, but I was grateful he took your mind off Todd. You were in a terrible state, Daddy and I were frantic. Fabian is effeminate, granted, but only seems dull because he can't offer you any passion. He'd be a hoot to keep as a pal. I can't believe you never noticed he's a friend of Dorothy. Last Christmas when *The Sound of Music* was on telly - again, he knew the words to every song. I thought he would leap onto the table when 'Climb Every Mountain' came on.'

'And he often sings 'Lonely Goatherd' when he's in the shower, Mummy. And when he's sad, it's 'Where is Love?' from *Oliver*.'

'You see! And you hate girly decor, but your house is a shrine to floribunda. I know none of it was your choice: When you got back from boarding school one Easter you went mad because we'd redecorated your bedroom with daisy wallpaper, and matching curtains. You said it was twee and insisted on stylish stripes instead.'

'Don't remind me, those daisies were horrifically twee. I don't know what you were thinking.'

'When you gloomed through your Goth stage, you had an all-black bedroom. The house you live in with Fabian would put the Chelsea Flower Show in the shade.'

Portia takes a large glug of wine. 'Oh, I feel foolish. It suited me not to notice, but this is funny, go on, what else?'

'When you were discussing getting a dog, Fabian wanted a Chihuahua, and you wanted a wolfhound. The swimming trunks he wears to our summer barbecues are about two sizes too small: Most enjoyable. He plucks his eyebrows, wears fake tan, and has perfectly manicured nails. I saw him eyeing up Mellows, our gardener, although I can't say I blame him, he's rather a hunk.'

Portia nearly chokes on a scallop. 'Mummy, behave!'

'Darling, I could go on and on. Daddy and I think it's a hoot and wondered when you'd notice. We'll support you whatever you do. Shall I treat you to Glampington Health Resort for a few weeks, to get over the shock?'

'No, I'm fine, but thanks, you and Pater do enough. I'll sort myself out, with help from someone called Izzie Firecracker.'

'Super, darling, shall we order dessert, and then you can tell me all about this fire-eater person.'

'Oh, Mummy, you're always getting words mixed up. It's *Firecracker*. And yes to dessert, but something naughty, I'm fed up of being reserved and careful, let's have sticky toffee pudding with ice-cream.'

'Well, I was going to suggest the sorbet selection, but, yes, let's indulge in comfort food. I can make up for it on the Stairmaster tomorrow. You should see my gym instructor, what a stud muffin; he makes me weak at the knees. Antoine wouldn't stand a chance if Fabian saw him.'

'Mummy, you're awful!'

Izzie moves to London, 1983

IZZIE WANTED TO GET to London as soon as possible. If she didn't go quickly, she'd be trapped in a bland existence forever.

She phoned Chantelle's London office and asked for a transfer.

'Maybe we can find you something in about six months.'

'No, I want to go next week.'

There was a long silence, followed by a doubtful, 'Well, there *is* a part-time vacancy in Selfingtons, but we can't offer you anything full-time at the moment.'

'I'll take it.'

A week later, on a hot Saturday morning in July, a girl from work, Sally, picked Izzie up in her dad's Granada Estate. She was off to visit her photographer brother, Willie Flash, in Camden. Sally helped load the luggage into the boot. There wasn't much. Izzie had given away most of her possessions, ready for a new start and Tim was selling the house contents: And the house.

Tim was dull but trustworthy, and she knew he'd send every last penny. He was the perfect husband for someone who wanted stability and routine. And who liked making lists, and buying bargain baked beans.

Once packed, she locked up the house and car, as per Tim's explicit instructions, wondering if he'd come and say goodbye. He didn't; maybe it wasn't on the short-term list. *Say goodbye to my soon to be ex-wife.* She posted all the keys through the letterbox and moved towards her new life.

After about four miles they made a detour, to say goodbye to her parents and brothers.

Izzie's older brother wasn't in. 'Treats this place like a hotel,' muttered her dad.

'Be quiet, Stanley,' ordered Rose. 'He's gone over to Liverpool to buy the *Murmur* album, by R.E.M. - I can't wait to hear it.'

'Neither can I,' agreed Izzie's little brother, looking away from another rerun of *Dad's Army*.

If it hadn't been for Izzie's older brother, her mum and dad would still be listening to Guy Mitchell singing 'Sparrow in the Treetop'. Instead, there was a vast library of albums at their disposal. When Rose went to the shops, she could talk about Bob Dylan, Jimi Hendrix, The Byrds and many more, while others discussed the price of sprouts.

Rose's favourite album was *Songs for Beginners*, by Graham Nash and she often danced around the living room to the 'Military Madness' track. But she still loved her childhood favourites and liked to sing Deanna Durbin songs as she washed dishes.

'Bye bye,' said Izzie. 'I must go; my friend is in the car.'

'Oh, I'm so worried about you. What happens if you get involved with drugs?' Rose said in a high-pitched tone.

'Don't worry; I promise to share them with you. Call you when I get there.'

And they were off. Turning onto the M6, heading south, 'Uptown Girl' came on the radio, and they sang along at the tops of their voices.

Izzie had lied to her parents and told them she was sharing a flat near Harrods with the sister of a friend from work.

The truth was she'd booked a room at Grotley Hostel on Tottenham Court Road, and planned to flat hunt from there.

It turned out she didn't stay at Grotley Palace for long. It was a London paved with metaphorical gold.

ONE EVENING, TWO DAYS after Izzie moved into her palatial new abode, Sally turned up at the door. 'I'm worried about you living in this awful place. My brother is downstairs and is taking us out. Hurry up, get your glad rags on, it'll be fun.'

Izzie was elated, saved from a feast of sardines on toast, put together in the depressing communal kitchen.

The evening was bliss. First, they went to Currying Flavour on Queensway for dinner. It was enormous fun, and the food delicious. Then they moved on to a hip and funky basement club, the Gangster's Moll on the King's Road.

At first, the nightclub was a bit slow, and the chat stilted. But it looked like things might liven up as Willie Flash took a large table, telling the waitress more people would join them. Two bottles of Bollinger and eight glasses soon arrived.

At about this time Izzie would be with Tim while he drank hot milk and munched toast and marmalade, cosy in paisley brushed-cotton pyjamas. She'd have a cup of tea to keep him company. She hates heated milk unless it has plenty of coffee in it, blaming it on the free milk for state school children she endured as a child. Yes, an excellent idea, but trying to drink it, when it has sat outside most of the morning in summer was the stuff of nightmares. She still shudders at the thought of the hideous sour beverage.

The club had a formal air and Izzie almost, for a millisecond, longed to be home with Tim. She couldn't have been more wrong.

A lively group soon joined them - a fashion designer, with his stunning model girlfriend, the two owners of the club and a charismatic man, called Jack: Izzie found him hilarious, he lit up the room and lifted the atmosphere from austere to joyful.

Jack and Izzie got on well. He laughed when she told him where she was living and sang 'Y.M.C.A.' at the top of his voice.

When he asked her out for dinner she nearly said no; he resembled a sandy-haired walrus. Then she remembered what a mistake she'd made, lured by Tim's handsome face and agreed to go.

The next evening, he picked her up from the hostel in a convertible Mercedes. A week later she moved in with him. It was a dramatic contrast from grotty Grotley - a decadent four-storey house in Notting Hill, complete with a small swimming pool in the basement.

IZZIE VISITED HER FAMILY one weekend and told everyone about her new London life, and Jack. Rose asked what he did for a living.

'He's a salesman; he sells tills to clubs.'

Rose's voice was tense: 'He sounds more like Jack the Lad to me. Come home at once. I don't want you living with a shady character.'

'As long as he's not Jack the Ripper, I don't see the problem,' soothed Stan.

Izzie was baffled. 'What do you mean, Mum, what are you upset about?'

'I won't have you living with a drug dealer.'

'Where did you get that idea?'

'You said he sells pills to clubs.'

'No, I didn't, I said he sells tills to clubs'

Her big brother laughed as he lovingly picked up an album, pulled the LP out of its sleeve and carefully placed it on the turntable. The sweet voice of Jennifer Warnes filled the room, singing 'Famous Blue Raincoat'.

Izzie wondered where her little brother was.

'He's gone to Liverpool to see *Monty Python's Meaning of Life* with a friend,' said Rose. 'I don't know what you all find so funny about that silly circus show, or whatever its stupid name is. And I'm still worried about this cash register business. It sounds dodgy. How can anyone sell enough tills to live in such a flamboyant house? There must be drugs involved.'

'Mum, he sells massive amounts of them, tills, not drugs, to pubs, clubs, restaurants, and just about anywhere that needs them. He even supplies museums. Come down and stay with us for a few days, check him out for yourself, and don't forget your swimsuit.'

Rose loved London and arrived the next week. She liked Jack, which surprised Izzie, who thought her mum would find him a bit racy.

'I recommend the steak and kidney pudding,' he told Izzie's mum, as they perused a menu. 'And have a drop of champers along with it.'

Rose, a life teetotaller, allowed herself a tiny glass of bubbly: She had been warned he was a good salesperson.

JACK DIDN'T WANT ANY rent from Izzie, but she still wanted to pay her way sometimes, tricky on a part-time salary. She was relieved to receive a cheque in the post from Tim; their marital abode had sold.

The cheque was for six thousand and three pounds; a small fortune to Izzie in the early 80's. Well, it would have been if she wasn't in London, keeping up with a champagne lifestyle.

At least it took the pressure off; she could afford to buy some decent clothes and had a fabulous time shopping. She bought a few carefully chosen basics in Way Out of Kensington, supplementing them with lots of fun and funky pieces from Top Girl.

Jack loved the new clothes and surprised her with a gift voucher for a posh boutique on South Molton Street, which, of course, was equipped with his cash registers. She chose a beautiful lightweight cashmere black coat with pink collar and cuffs. Excited, she phoned Jack at work to tell him about it. He arrived home in the early hours, as usual. Izzie was in bed.

'Don't you like your new coat?'

'Of course, I do!'

'Then why aren't you wearing it?'

FOR A FEW WEEKS AFTER the windfall, Jack would introduce her thus: 'This is Izzie. She's got six thousand and three pounds.'

Then the divorce came through, and she was ecstatic, she didn't want to marry Jack, but freedom felt good.

Izzie loved London life and thought she'd arrived.

Or had she?

After a while, Izzie got tired of the endless socialising and longed for the contrast of a few quiet evenings at home, watching a video or reading, and having a simple dinner. She tried staying in for a rest some evenings, but that often didn't work as planned, not with parties going on most nights, some revellers still there when she left to catch the tube to work.

One morning there was a man called Cliff, walking around the living room in circles saying, 'Where am I going to go, what am I going to do, who am I going to talk to?' He repeated the phrase over and over, wearing the carpet bare as he circled. He hadn't slept and was in the full throes of post cocaine paranoia. Scarily, he was a dentist, about to leave for work. Izzie was glad she wasn't his patient.

The price of cocaine was high, about sixty pounds a gram. Nevertheless, Jack and his friends always had a supply in their wallets, and some of the girls who draped themselves around the house kept some stashed in their handbags.

WORKING IN SELFINGTONS, Izzie met a fun girl called Zelda, who was engaged to a man from Canada. She and Izzie got on brilliantly and lunched together most days. They were making the most of their time together as Zelda was about to be married and was moving to Ontario.

'What do you want for a wedding present, Zel?'

'Oh, Iz, would you score us a gram of coke from the night-club you go to on the King's Road? We want a rock n roll few days in the hotel suite after the wedding, with wild sex and de-bauchery.'

'Wouldn't you like a nice decanter?'

'Ha, bloody ha, no!'

Izzie was horrified but didn't want to be a wimp or a killjoy. A week before the wedding, a bundle of nerves, and armed with sixty quid, she sneaked into the Gangster's Moll and approached an emaciated, pallid, rat-faced man, who, apparently, always had 'the goods' on him. Could he be a plainclothes police officer? Surely not, looking like that; the police force would have to be desperate. He thankfully wasn't and slipped Izzie a small folded envelope.

Until she could safely hand over the gift, Izzie felt like a criminal. Maybe the man who'd slipped her the package *was* a detective. She kept the contraband hidden in her underwear drawer, but on the Friday before the wedding had to take 'the goods' into Selfingtons as she was catching the train to Sussex for the wedding, straight from work. She popped the package in her handbag, feeling scared.

On the way out of Oxford Street tube station, a hand grabbed her shoulder. 'You're under arrest.'

Izzie's throat dried, and her heart pounded.

'Ha-ha!'

It was Malcolm from work, also off to the wedding, with his boyfriend. Over lunch in the Stewpot the day before she'd told him all about the gift and her terror about getting into trouble.

'I'll kill you, Malcolm,' said Izzie.

'I wonder if I have the CIA onto me. I bought them a bottle of tequila, and it's in my suitcase.'

'Bugger off!'

'If only, darling!'

FINALLY, THE NEXT DAY, in the ladies of an exclusive country hotel Izzie handed over the packet. Zelda lifted up her wedding dress and calmly slipped the envelope into a stocking top.

Izzie would never make a drug-runner.

The next week she was having lunch in Blossoms with a friend from work, Christine, who said, 'Hey, don't look now and make it obvious, but the man at the corner table looks like a typical drug dealer.'

Izzie surreptitiously peeked and saw her cocaine supplier. 'That's because he is. Well spotted.'

Christine sniggered. 'Bloody hell, I'm observant. He must be the guy you bought the wedding gift from.'

'The very same, you should be a detective. Cagney and Lacey have got nothing on you. Have you ever tried drugs?'

'No, but I make up for it with copious amounts of wine. What about you?'

'I've snorted coke with Jack about three times but got paranoid, anxious and depressed. I had terrible anxiety nightmares where everything went wrong. One night, I dreamed I was homeless, pushing around my few belongings in a shopping trolley.'

'I'll definitely stick with the old vino. I've got too many clothes; they'd never fit in a shopping cart.'

Logically Izzie knew what caused the nightmare: She and Jack paid another visit to Currying Flavour for dinner. This time they were joined by two models, ex-girlfriends of Jack's. On the way home he spotted an abandoned shopping trolley and told the duo to get in, and he would chauffeur them home. A curious policeman came along: 'What is going on here, Sir?'

'Well, it's like this, Officer. I spotted these models, two for the price of one, in the supermarket and I'm wheeling them home.'

The young policeman tried to look serious, without success. 'Well, on you go, Sir, but be careful.'

Yes, it was a fantastic contrast to her former life, but Izzie was running out of money, the windfall from the house dwindling fast and the novelty of life with Jack wearing off: He was too much. Izzie was exhausted and looked dreadful, with dull skin, eye bags and dark shadows. No amount of the expensive skin-care available to her made much difference. She still looked like hell and needed more sleep.

Instead of fantasising about the high-life she dreamed of early nights, snuggled up in bed with a novel. Had it been a mistake to leave Tim? She shook herself. No, it was not. It's scary how lack of sleep can affect us.

ONE SATURDAY AFTER yet another late night she staggered into Selfingtons and was falling asleep at the counter. All she could focus on was the morning break when she planned to eat an enormous greasy breakfast in the staff canteen, washed down with a massive mug of builder's tea.

'What on earth is wrong with you?' asked Honey Potts, another part-timer and a new friend.

'I'm knackered and can't stand living with Jack anymore. It's driving me nuts. I need to find a full-time job and my own flat, in that order.'

'Don't be daft,' Honey surprised her. 'Come and live with me. I'd love it.'

'Oh my God, are you serious? That'd be amazing. When can I come along and how much is the rent?'

'Move in next Monday if you want and as for the cost...'

She named a minuscule amount, and Izzie decided there and then to move to Eastling Square the next week. A posh address; Honey Potts was the mistress of a rich, and ancient, sugar daddy.

'And, you're so tired you can hardly stand up, darling. Lie down in front of the lipstick drawer and have a little sleep. I'll keep my eye out for the floor manager,' added Honey.

Izzie was a coward and didn't tell Jack she was leaving. Luckily, she was due a day off the next Monday, and as soon as he'd gone to the office, she piled her stuff into a suitcase and some bin liners and called a cab.

She was off again.

Honey Potts

HONEY ORGANISED HER social life meticulously as there were so many men to juggle, along with the sugar daddy who paid for the flat and most expenses.

Izzie couldn't believe what she witnessed on a day off. Honey had dates for lunch, afternoon tea, early dinner and late dinner. And we aren't talking about fruit - although they were probably juicy meetings.

Yes, four men in one day. Each suitor picked Honey up from home, so the *man*oeuvres were farcical. Izzie felt like a nun or Victorian governess in comparison. She'd be taking up embroidery or tapestry next.

Honey flew through the door after each encounter for a quick breather, loo visit, hair brush, teeth clean and makeup redo.

Izzie was amazed and rather impressed. 'How do you get rid of them, before the next one comes along?'

'Easily, I say Mum will be here at whatever o'clock and doesn't know I have a boyfriend. As if. Oh, God. There's the doorbell again. Please get it, Izzie, while I pop my lippy on and nip to the loo? Tell him to wait in the car.'

Izzie opened the door to find an anxious man, florid-faced, in about his mid-forties. He wasn't the sugar daddy, but one of the younger ones. 'Honey will be out in a sec and wondered if you'd wait in the car.'

'Honey mistreats me, but I adore her. It's not fair. What can I do to make her love me?' His eyes welled with tears.

'Maybe you should stop crying. Quick, chin up, shoulders back, take a deep breath. Spit spot.'

'Do you sleep with them all?' Izzie asked.

'Oh no darling, not usually, only the sugar daddy, he's late dinner today.'

Izzie couldn't understand why Honey wasn't fat with the endless restaurant visits. However, she was a size twelve, statuesque and curvy. Her hair was long and blonde; the colour courtesy of an expensive salon, Anthony and Man of Sloane Square, not inherited from her mum. Honey was the child of a small plain-faced fat woman, whose idea of dressing up was removing her apron. Honey despaired whenever the sugar daddy invited her mum to dinner.

'It's embarrassing, Izzie. When she goes out with Dad, they never have starters, just a main course and a shared dessert, with tap water to drink. When we take her out, she goes through the menu: starter, main course with wine, dessert, cheese, coffee and brandy: Every darn time.'

Rose deserved a load of Brownie points; she would never do that.

IZZIE WAS RELIEVED to find Honey was human, and indulged in crash-out and do-nothing days.

'Oh darling, I'm tired. Be an angel - go and get fish and chips. And some wine. Let's slob out and watch *Monty Python's Life of Brian.*'

Who could refuse such a perfect combination? Not Izzie, who bumped into a nosy neighbour, Mr Parker, when she was off to work the day after *Python* and chips.

'Good morning, Miss. I saw a Rolls Royce, a Mercedes and an Aston Martin outside your flat the other day.'

'Not surprising,' said Izzie; it would hardly be a fleet of Robin Reliants turning up at the salubrious address.

A four-date day was a rare occurrence; Honey usually kept to only two liaisons, early dinner and late: Frugality in the extreme. Izzie wondered what it reminded her of, ah, yes, first and second sittings in the dining hall at Butlin's. The sugar daddy was generally on Honey's early shift so he could get back to his wife.

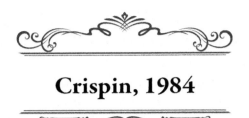

Crispin, 1984

IZZIE WAS STILL A BEAUTY consultant, but full-time. The divorce money was gone. London was scarily expensive. She was excited to receive a letter from Tim, who sometimes sent funds after sales of joint possessions. The proceeds from the sale of the video player had been a pleasant surprise and paid for a fabulous new outfit. She tore open the envelope:

DEAR IZZIE,

I hope you're happy in London. I've got a new girlfriend, Susan, who is a receptionist at Crypt's Funeral Directors. I have sold the standard lamp. Here's a cheque for £4.53, half the proceeds.

Love,
Tim

A PALTRY AMOUNT BUT Izzie appreciated the honesty. What the heck, a funeral parlour, must be dead quiet in there. Maybe livelier than life with Tim, though.

Via Jack's best mate Izzie discovered he was hurt when she upped and left but partly relieved to be free to return to a playboy existence. Izzie missed Jack and his wonderful sense of humour and phoned to apologise. 'It was horrible of me to leave without telling you, I'm sorry.'

'You're forgiven. You did cramp my style a bit when you lived with me, and the phone bill was mega.'

They began seeing each other again, on a casual basis. Jack was generous, under the circumstances, and loaned her one of the company vehicles. To return the favour she spent half a day a week delivering tills. The car was nothing fancy, although she loved buzzing around London in the cute yellow Renault 5.

One evening they arranged to meet for the fortieth birthday party of one of Jack's old schoolmates, at Racy's nightclub in Belgravia.

Jack didn't turn up: Phoning him, Izzie discovered he was in bed with his Night Nurse. Unfortunately, it was out of a bottle, not the real McCoy. Cindy had fulfilled her childhood dream of becoming a nurse and was working in a London hospital. Jack nearly needed a defibrillator when she came over to the house in her uniform, after work one evening.

'Are you sure you can't drag yourself out of bed, Jack?'

'Izzie, even if Hugh Hefner was throwing the party, I couldn't make it. I just want to stay here and die.'

Although Izzie felt a little sorry for the invalid, not having an escort was no problem: She'd never worried about going to events alone, even as young as five, and adored the big-skirted party dresses little girls wore in the sixties. At the time Izzie loved them and the frillier, the better.

Because of a cold, her mum once made her wear a hand-knitted woollen suit for a school Christmas bash, with a vest and liberty bodice underneath. The horror! Izzie felt like the ugly duckling, watching the other little girls in their froufrou dresses, and hated every minute of the party.

For this 1980's shindig, she decided against a frilly dress or a hand-knitted suit and opted for tight black stirrup pants, and a bright blue lacy jumper with dangling diamante jewels around the neckline; one of Honey's designer castoffs. Izzie felt fabulous. She knew a few of the other guests and spent a pleasant evening floating about with a champagne glass, which was filled at regular intervals: Bliss.

Towards the end of the night, a nice-looking man, with dark hair and eyes, said, 'Hello, I'm Crispin, fancy a drink?'

'That's generous, seeing as all the beverages are on the house, but yes, please.' She knew it sounded a tad rude, but felt strangely nervous.

Crispin instantly procured two fresh glasses of bubbly and two seats in the packed nightclub.

They sat chatting for a while, the conversation flowing. It turned out Crispin earned even less than Izzie, so it was a surprise when he suggested lunch in a stylish restaurant in St Christopher's Place the next day. Result! Apart from anything, it'd be a treat to avoid the staff canteen. And, he was cute.

THE NEXT MORNING, SHE half-heartedly sold lipsticks and anti-wrinkle creams to optimists while anticipating Crispin's arrival. She'd asked him to wait outside, but he said he preferred to meet her at the counter, which meant she couldn't sneak off without telling anyone. Drat!

Crispin was punctual, at the appointed time of one o'clock he appeared through the revolving doors, like a genie from a lamp.

The counter manager did a low wolf whistle. 'Wow. Your date is cute, and lovely and tall. I'll have him if you change your mind.'

'Shut up, he'll hear you,' hissed Izzie.

Crispin had worn casual clothes the night before, giving the appearance of an overgrown schoolboy. Now, in a tailored grey suit, pink shirt, purple silk tie and elegant grey fedora hat, he looked older, more his real age of thirty.

'I'll meet you at the staff entrance; I'm not supposed to use the main one,' said Izzie.

Crispin raised an eyebrow as if to say what a ridiculous rule, and what a silly little person you are for obeying it. 'Well, you should have said.'

She had, but not to worry.

The restaurant was Italian and cosy. Not the typical sandwich bar affair she and her co-workers sometimes enjoyed as a canteen alternative. It was impressive and somewhat generous, considering Crispin's low income.

It was a pleasant, light-hearted lunch, chatting away, enjoying pasta and glasses of Valpolicella. A mere hour couldn't do such an excellent restaurant justice, and all too soon it was time to go back to work.

As they finished their espressos, Crispin said, 'I hope you'll do me a favour. I was on holiday in the States a few months ago and got a little tipsy one evening. I told two girls due to backpack around Europe that they could stay with me for a night or two. They're meant to be arriving this evening, and I can't stand the thought of it. I wonder if you'd pretend to be my live-in girlfriend, to make it easier to get rid of them. Can I pick you up from work?'

'What about the girls, they may not find anywhere else to stay on such short notice.'

'Oh don't worry. I've got a friend who's agreed to put them up.'

'Oh, well why not?' Izzie cheered inwardly but was miffed she'd still be in her boring uniform. She had no clothes with her to change into, payday was a week away, and the six thousand and three pounds a happy distant memory.

AFTER AN ENDLESS AFTERNOON selling more makeup and skincare six o'clock arrived and Izzie headed for the staff entrance, red lipstick and musky fragrance reapplied, looking forward to meeting Crispin. She didn't see him at first and thought he was late, or she'd been stood up, then spotted him beckoning from over the road. 'Come on, this way. The car is around the corner.'

Izzie expected a battered run-around. Instead there stood a gleaming and exquisite grey vintage Bentley.

'Is this yours? I thought you earned less than me?'

'Ha! The paltry salary just about pays for petrol: I also have a private income. Thank God.'

Izzie was both pleased and disappointed. Jack and most of his friends were wealthy, and it was hard to keep up. It was one reason her divorce money disappeared so fast.

Honey thought she was nuts. 'Don't be silly, Izzie, I never pay for a thing when I'm with a man. I buy him the occasional tie, and that's fine.'

But Honey treated her dog, Lady Penelope, like an empress: The poodle slept in a four-poster bed from Pampered Pooch of Knightsbridge. The arrival of a doggy sedan chair in the green and gold delivery van wouldn't have surprised Izzie.

Honey adored her precious pet and hated leaving her alone. She always turned the radio or television on and called at least once a day when she was out. Does this mean Lady Penelope picked up the phone with a paw? No, but Honey would leave messages on the answerphone. 'Hello, darling, it's Mummy. Are you having a lovely day? I'll be home soon with a treat, and then we'll go for a nice walk. Goodbye Penny Poodle Pops. I love you.'

'I have less than a dog's life and have to beg for attention,' lamented the sugar daddy.

'Maybe you should grow long ears,' teased Izzie.

Honey sashayed into the room on a cloud of Chantelle Number Eight, a heady combination of jasmine and vanilla. 'What are you two laughing at?'

'Woof woof!' barked Izzie.

'Cow! You played Lady Penelope's messages. I'll get you back. Come on, Cyril. Let's go.'

So, that's the sugar daddy's name, mused Izzie, giggling at the thought of yelling *Oh, Cyril!* in the throes of faux passion. Honey had her in hysterics one evening re-enacting her fake orgasms. Lady Penelope joined in with the howls, which made it even funnier.

SINCE ARRIVING IN LONDON, Izzie noticed that many wealthy people had little comprehension of what it's like to live on an average income. Going out for meals, buying new clothes and going to the cinema were everyday normalities. She got swept up in the same expensive social whirl, and it was hard to keep up.

When she met a friend pre-London, they might have chatted over wine, coffee or both. Sometimes, as a treat, or on someone's birthday, they'd eat out. Occasionally they invited each other to their homes for dinner. In the decadent 80's London of Izzie's experience, most of her friends never stayed home in the evenings, unless it was to recover from several nights out in a row. Dining in restaurants and sometimes heading off to nightclubs afterwards was the norm.

A woman she met had never turned on the oven she'd owned for two years: 'Oh, darling, I can't be bothered to read the instructions. It's much easier to dine out, and there's no washing up.'

'Haven't you got a dishwasher?' asked Izzie.

'Oh, yes, I use it to wash champagne glasses and the dog's bowl.'

Izzie didn't want to appear stingy by not offering to pay sometimes, but the cost of drinks, meals or both was eye-wateringly steep.

'Oh, let's have another bottle of champers, Izzie, darling.'

'I'll have the Dover sole, off the bone.'

'Shall we start with a few oysters?'

'You can't go wrong with a Chateauneuf du Pape.'

'Is asparagus still in season?'

What happened to plonk de plonk, or half a lager and a packet of crisps?

Was it fun? Yes. Was it kind to her bank account? No.

Izzie had been a tad relieved when she thought Crispin was at a similar financial level as herself, and they could rise through the ranks side by side. It was not to be, although not everyone Izzie met was wealthy.

Lots of the girls she worked with had similar lifestyles to the type she'd shared with Tim, but maybe not as dull. Although there was one girl who was always so broke she couldn't afford a topping on her baked potato when they ate at the local budget cafe, the Stewpot, and ordered it plain, with butter, along with a glass of Eau de Tap.

CRISPIN PACKED OFF the backpackers to the friend's house in a taxi, soon after they arrived. Izzie pretended to be the live-in girlfriend, hamming it up like crazy. 'We only met last month, but it was love at first sight, wasn't it, Crispy? We can't bear to be apart, even for one night.'

Afterwards, 'Crispy' took her home to change, and waited outside in the car, before they went to Wok this Way in Chelsea, for dinner, where a waiter showed her how to eat with chopsticks. Izzie and Crispin enjoyed a fabulous evening and after that went on regular dates.

Jack and Crispin knew about each other, and it suited them all not to feel tied down. Izzie felt free but being broke spoilt things. Crispin was like royalty and never seemed to carry cash.

'Tip, the doorman, darling.'

'Fill the parking meter will you.'

'I've got no cash to tip the waiter, have you got a few quid?'

'The opera singer chap in the basement flat is home from Russia and has cheap caviar for sale. Have you got twenty quid to buy a tin? I thought I'd have it for my packed lunch tomorrow.'

'Can't you have luncheon meat or egg and cress, like everyone else?' said Izzie.

Apart from his lack of readies, Crispin was generous with things he could pay for by cheque.

However, he didn't appear to notice all the bits and bobs she paid for, as they were such trifles; even the caviar. Over a dinner, he said, 'I'm stony broke this week and can't afford the new white wall tyres I want for my Bentley.'

One evening Izzie blew a week's wages to treat him to dinner at an expensive restaurant; Roux Sauce, in Parliament Square. Crispin was flippant about it, and when the waiter took the order said, 'Tell the chef we're in a hurry.'

Izzie was livid. 'For God's sake, we're not in a greasy spoon. I don't want to spend all this money to rush the experience. What's your hurry?'

'I want to get home in time for *Star Trek*.'

A week later they were in the Lilac Rooms cafe in Barnes, having tea and scones, and he acted like a guest in a five-star hotel. She thought he was rude to the waitress. 'You're behaving like the lord of the manor, Crispin.'

In her young mind, there were two choices in life: It was this or a Tim-like dull existence.

No contest.

Crispin couldn't relate to the concept of eating at home. Izzie kept saying it would be a pleasant change to stay in one evening, so he offered to cook.

Arriving at his flat, a tantalising aroma of a soon-to-be-ready roast dinner made her tummy grumble. Her mouth watered imagining roast potatoes, fluffy on the inside, crisp on the outside. Maybe she'd be naughty and add lashings of butter. Crispin gave her a glass of red wine and told her dinner would be ready soon, and then disappeared into the kitchen.

Ten minutes later he appeared, carrying a silver platter bearing three racks of lamb, coated in honey and mustard, placing it on the table with a flourish. Then he disappeared and came back again with two warmed plates and a carving knife. He lit the candles in the candelabra, switched off the lights, sat down and poured himself a glass of wine. 'Cheers, Izzie and bon appétit. He put an entire rack of lamb on his plate and began to devour it. A few bites in he paused, looking puzzled. 'Izzie, why aren't you eating?'

'I'm waiting for the veggies, roast potatoes and gravy.'

'There aren't any. I only cooked lamb; it's my favourite. I could eat it every night.'

'Will there be any pudding?'

'I thought we'd go out for coffee and dessert.'

In Wharton's bar in Barking Square a week later Crispin invited a friend to his flat for breakfast the next morning. He'd enjoyed the novelty of dining at home and wanted to expand the experience.

'What will you serve him?' Izzie asked. 'You've only got cola and guinea fowl in the fridge.'

'That's what he's having.'

A few years later Izzie bumped into the unfortunate recipient of the morning repast. 'I couldn't believe it. There I was, looking forward to bacon and eggs with a pot of tea and I had guinea fowl and cola. I still feel sick thinking about it.'

JACK WON THE SALESMAN of the Year award, and the prize was a three-week holiday for two in Jamaica. He asked Izzie to go with him. Apart from her lacklustre honeymoon with Tim, she'd never left the UK and couldn't say no to a free trip to the Caribbean. But Chantelle refused her the time off. She thought they'd understand about the holiday of a lifetime, but the more she tried to talk them round the more adamant they became.

Izzie begged one last time. 'I'm sorry, but I can't bear to refuse the holiday, I'm going anyway. I'll willingly take time off without pay.'

The voice at the other end of the phone was angry: 'Izzie, you are not listening - the answer was, and is, no.'

When she got back to the counter, looking furious and close to tears the others knew she'd had no joy.

'The meanies,' said the counter-manager. 'Go on the holiday, I would, but don't tell them I said so. I'll do my best to talk them around while you're away. Want to borrow any bikinis; we're about the same size?'

'And I've got loads,' said Honey.

Izzie flew to the Caribbean, with a suitcase full of swimwear.

JACK ARRIVED AT THE exotic location and beautiful hotel and said, 'Right: beach, sea, palm trees - done it. Where's the bar?'

He wasn't joking. They enjoyed excellent dinners every evening, with an abundance of wine and cocktails for Jack, and one Pina Colada for Izzie. She was limiting herself so she'd be fresh enough to enjoy daytimes in paradise. Izzie was free to swim, read or stroll along endless white beaches. Jack spent most of the days recovering from hangovers.

One day Izzie enjoyed a long walk along the water's edge, accompanied by her Walkman. When Stevie Wonder sang 'A Place in the Sun', she was in heaven.

The hotel manager told them a special dinner was being arranged in their honour and to come to reception at 8 pm.

After Jack's first cocktail of the evening, and his umpteenth of the day, they were lead to the water's edge. A table for two awaited, with a white linen tablecloth, candles, ice bucket, the works. The chef cooked lobster on a barbecue and a waiter was in constant attendance. A steel band played 'Yellow Bird' and other songs, just for them. How many tills had Jack sold, for God's sake?

The meal was divine, the wine sublime and it should have been a perfect evening. But it felt wrong, incongruous; she and Jack didn't belong in a romantic setting together. She'd rather be in an everyday environment with someone who rocked her world. Although she and Jack had fun, the holiday underlined her intuition they weren't right for each other, their relationship was a fun fling and an excellent antidote to the stifling years with Tim.

Removing any doubt at the far nooks and crannies of Izzie's mind, Jack was sick on the beach as they headed back to their villa: Twice.

In the main, it was a fabulous holiday, but arriving back in London there were some unhappy surprises.

Although Jack said he hadn't minded Izzie phoning Crispin from the hotel, he was upset and didn't want to see her again. He asked for the car back.

And there were two unwelcome letters.

IZZIE,

As it seems OK for you to go on an exotic trip at a moment's notice, I'm sure you won't mind me doing the same. I'm flying out to LA to meet up with a friend, and we're off globe-trotting from there. See you in about three months, maybe.

Crispin x

DEAR IZZIE,

Although your counter-manager has spoken in your defence, we are shocked you have so little respect for the company that you would go on holiday with inadequate notice and without permission.

Please consider this letter your official notice of termination. Your severance cheque is enclosed.

Mrs Petty,
Chantelle Head Office.

Izzie, jobless & single, 1985

SO THERE IZZIE WAS, at Honey's, single and jobless. She felt a mixture of dread and excitement but realised how much she would miss Crispin. She'd been a stupid, selfish cow and had got her comeuppance.

Honey was sympathetic. 'I can fix you up with one of my men. You could be set up in a flat, like me.'

'No, thanks most of them are the same age as my dad, or older. I doubt there are any as young and good looking as Tom Cruise.'

'What's wrong with that? They're rich, so what's the problem?'

'It doesn't matter to you, but it does to me. I can't help imagining what your men would look like when those expensive, well-tailored suits come off.'

'Well, it's not often good. I close my eyes and think of diamonds. Last night when the sugar daddy was huffing away on top of me, and asphyxiating me with oniony breath, I imagined an entire treasure chest of sparkling jewels.'

It was fun living with Honey, and Izzie knew how lucky she was. She was only paying twenty pounds a week to share the luxury pad, cheaper than the utilitarian room at the hostel, but soon she wouldn't even be able to afford that. More funds were needed, and fast. She had a brainwave and phoned Jack.

Izzie's idea was to have a change from cosmetics. She knew a group of girls who'd come down from Liverpool to work in Stringham's Nightclub in Covent Garden as cocktail waitresses and earned a fortune in tips. She planned to join them.

The next day, over a glass of wine in Blossoms Cafe, Izzie put the idea to Jack.

He said nothing.

'Jack?'

'There is no way you're working as a cocktail waitress.'

'Why? I could earn lots of money. And you know everyone; I bet Stringham's has your tills.'

'Of course, it does. But it's not for you. I can read people. How do you think I'm such a good salesman? You'd hate it. Your favourite thing is going to bed early with a good book. How on earth would you manage to get to work at eight and leave at four the next morning? Plus, you hate cocaine, and it's the only way most of them cope with the hours. Trust me; I've dated a few cocktail waitresses.'

Now, there's a surprise.

'But I need money, Jack, and fast. I want to stay in London.'

'I do have another idea. What do you think of this fine establishment? I met the owner a few days ago, and he's looking for someone to greet and seat the punters. You'd be perfect.'

'Why?'

'Because you talk to everyone, you're a nutcase. Whenever you travel on a tube, train or bus you come back with a story of someone you met. It's not normal to get on the underground and chat away to people like they're old friends.'

Izzie laughed. 'That's pretty standard for anyone from my part of the world. It's you lot that's strange.'

'Well, do you want the job or not? You'll get a base wage and a percentage of the takings.'

'Hell, yes.'

IZZIE LOVED WORKING in Blossoms. Although the work was hard, it was almost like being paid to go out. However, she missed Crispin and refused all offers of dates, unless they were platonic. Secretly she wanted him back and would do nothing to sabotage the possibility. But for the first time in ages, she wasn't broke. Hurrah!

JIMMY WEST, AN EX-FOOTBALL star, came in most days, to drink numerous bottles of beer, either at his favourite corner table, with a few other regulars or at the bar, on his own. He missed his glory days, but always got a warm welcome in Blossoms, which emulated adulation from the crowds. His piercing blue eyes were beautiful, and his voice sweet-toned, like soothing music. He was a gentle, pleasant soul, and Izzie was fond of him, despite him being a man of few words, although he usually had something to whisper in her ear whenever he left; his address! She never took him up on the invitation. Anyway, he probably always forgot about his generous offer by the next day.

A QUIET, MIDDLE-AGED gentleman, Hector, visited once a week, usually ordering fettuttine carbonara and Sancerre, and sometimes asked Izzie to join him for a glass of wine. When the place was quiet, she did, and they got on well. He invited her out for lunch, and she agreed to go.

When they were breaking the tops of their crème brulees, he asked her to come to Paris with him for the weekend. Izzie was surprised at how naive she still was after a while in London, and even more to the point, living with Honey. She thought of Hector as a friend, but he apparently wanted more. Izzie said no to Paris; there was no way she wanted to be Honey Mark Two. She told Hector she'd love to carry on seeing him, as friends. To her delight, he said yes.

Their friendship became even better as Hector stopped being shifty about his home life and opened up about his wife and sons. Lunch became a happy regular appointment. One day he said, 'You should be a therapist or a motivational speaker. You seem to bring out the best in people; I've watched how the staff and customers respond to you.'

'Thanks, Hector.' It was a lovely compliment, which sewed a seed for the future.

'Thanks to you, too. My wife said I've been better company in the last few weeks. And one of my sons said I'm less of a miserable git, and wondered if I was on drugs.'

'I can score some coke if you want.' Izzie winked and told the tale of her intrepid visit to the Gangster's Moll.

WITHIN A FEW MONTHS, the owner of Blossoms promoted Izzie to the position of floor manager, meaning she was in charge of hiring and firing waiting staff, organising and overseeing their shifts and also, coordinating the laundering of tablecloths. The latter was a nightmare and so was firing someone, but luckily it only happened once, when she found a demure looking waitress smuggling out three bottles of wine and an entire carrot cake. But in the main Izzie loved the job and met some wonderful characters.

The owner, a bald pale-faced man called Dave, let her employ a deputy manager. Izzie chose a fun and attractive girl, Gronya, who she met working in Selfingtons.

Gronya was funny. 'Hey, Izzie; check out the skinny man on table twelve - doesn't he look like Zippy?'

He did.

Evenings and Sundays were the best times to work because the customers had time to linger over meals, making the atmosphere chilled. Izzie started putting candles on every table at dusk: She got a great deal on a huge job lot at the local candle factory, Flickers, in Battersea.

As a result, the ambience was sultry, relaxed and romantic, and Izzie revelled in it. One evening she sat chatting to one of her favourite customers, sipping wine, as the lovely flames danced and Phyllis Nelson sang 'Move Closer'. Perfect.

As a contrast, Saturday, after lunch was a manic nightmare and Izzie always woke up dreading it. Afternoon tea began at about three o'clock. The turnover was so fast there were never enough staff and tempers got fraught. Customers became agitated, asking where their teas, coffees, cakes and scones were. Izzie begged Dave for extra staff to cover the dreaded afternoons. He refused.

Every Saturday she wanted to scream and run far away. One day she ran out the back door and stood in the yard saying, 'Beam me up, Scotty.' Unfortunately, it didn't work. She tried twitching her nose, like Samantha from *Bewitched*, which was equally ineffective. She headed back into the fray, amazed when a customer called her over and said, 'We are wondering how you do it, Miss Cool Cucumber. That's your new name.'

'Why?'

'We've been sitting here enjoying our cake, surprised you're so calm in this frantic environment.'

If they only knew: Confirmation indeed that appearances can be deceptive. At least after Saturday's mania, she looked forward to Sunday's calm and enjoyed choosing music for a laid-back, happy vibe.

Izzie's favourite Sunday lunch song was Louis Armstrong's 'Wonderful World'. It was followed by a few Doris Day tracks, on the reel-to-reel tape. When Calamity Jane started singing 'The Deadwood Stage', the cheery tune woke up the customers. One wit decided to use the cake trolley as a stagecoach. Tying a napkin about his head, in the style of a bonnet, he boarded the front, ruining a chocolate fudge cake. His mate was the driver and pushed the trolley up and down the cafe as the punters clapped, sang and whooped.

'Whip crack away!'

Izzie joined in for a while, then worried that Dave would make a surprise appearance and go mad. She knew he'd be livid about the safety aspect and annoyed about the wasted cake. Frankly, she thought him a misery, most of the time, and somewhat lazy.

Most Sundays he phoned to have his lunch delivered from the restaurant, and he only lived a mile away. Izzie would stand on the King's Road with a foil-covered plate, beckoning a taxi and then persuading the driver to act as a meal delivery service. She felt ridiculous.

'Can you take this to 22 Universal Road, please?'

'What do you think I am love, bleeding Meals on Wheels?'

'Please, I'll get into trouble from the boss if you don't.'

'Is he ill?'

'No.'

'Oh, alright then, but the lazy bastard had better give me a decent tip, or I'll scoff the lot.'

Izzie sighed with relief. 'Thanks.'

IN THE MAIN, THE FUN continued until it all went wrong after an unusually busy Friday evening when the revellers partied on until after midnight. Izzie and Gronya were exhausted after ushering out the last reluctant guest. They were dreaming of their duvets and couldn't wait to lock the door.

Izzie was due back in for a breakfast shift the next morning, at eight o'clock.

They were horrified to find something wrong with the lock and couldn't get it to work, despite trying for over half an hour, but didn't dare leave the place open and ended up staying the night, as impromptu security guards. The last thing they wanted.

Dave, the owner, wouldn't mind and would probably give them a medal for bravery.

They were wrong - he was furious and sacked them for being irresponsible.

Izzie trudged home feeling despondent, wronged and hurt. Flinging her coat on the sofa, she saw the answer phone light flashing. It was probably Honey leaving a message for Lady Penelope, but she pressed play, to be sure.

There were two messages. One was from a sheepish sounding Dave saying he'd overreacted after too much to drink, and asking her to come back. No, she couldn't face it. Dave was a despot: The week before he'd gone mad when she took two days off together after working ten days of double shifts straight. He'd balanced his rage with a compliment saying the restaurant didn't run the same when she wasn't there. But Izzie was starting to feel like a slave. On the other hand, she did enjoy the job, most of the time. What to do?

The second message was a big surprise: 'Hi Izzie, it's Crispin. I miss you, and I'm coming home. Let's get engaged.'

Saved by Alexander Graham Bell.

Or was she?

Izzie marries again

IZZIE MARRIED CRISPIN in September 1987. She thought the marriage would create her perfect life. She had a wealthy and attractive husband and was living in a luxurious flat in Knightsbridge.

Because of Crispin's private income, there were no money worries. They indulged in at least three long-haul holidays a year, with Crispin choosing the destinations. When in London they dined out several times a week. The social diary was full. They saw nearly every film shown within a five-mile radius.

Izzie was free to spend hours browsing in bookshops most days, buying as many books as she wanted. The icing on the cake was that Crispin loved early nights as much as she did: Even, or especially, when friends visited, he escaped to bed early, leaving Izzie to her hostess duties. 'My wife will entertain you. Goodnight.'

'But, we've only been here an hour,' said a bemused guest, one evening.

AT LEAST TWICE A MONTH they drove to Cambridge to visit Crispin's parents, William and Bea.

Unfortunately, Crispin's mum had a love-hate relationship with her daughter-in-law. On the 'love' days Izzie and Bea would chat away happily. On the 'hate' ones, Bea would make snide remarks about Izzie, both to her face and behind her back.

'Our solicitor saw you on Oxford Street the other day. He said you were wearing a short skirt.'

'I didn't see him.'

'Well, he saw you and was embarrassed.'

'Why?'

'It should be obvious, dear. You're far too old to wear a mini skirt. They make you look like a woman of ill repute; you *are* thirty.'

Bea's husband controlled her, and before marriage, her dad had ruled. She was always discouraged from making any life decisions for herself, or from getting a job.

'I bought myself a house once, Izzie, a little cottage when I inherited some money when a favourite aunt died. I loved it, so much more than this mausoleum. I don't like having staff; I'd rather have something to do. I'd like to make some of the meals, but William insists on the housekeeper doing the cooking, he says I over-season everything.'

Izzie was intrigued. 'What happened to the cottage?'

'My dad made me sell it; said I hadn't consulted him.'

Flipping heck thought Izzie. 'But surely you were married by then.'

'Yes, but I did what he said. I'm hopeless at standing up for myself. That's one of the reasons I like a drink; I can live in my dreams. Maybe I'd run away if I had enough of my own money.' Bea took a sip of champagne.

THE FAMILY ACCOUNTANT, Mr Ledger, came over to Izzie's in-laws for a meeting which included Crispin and his dad. Nipping to the loo, Izzie heard an alarming snippet of conversation coming from the study.

'I feel terrible about this,' said the accountant. 'Isn't it time to let Bea know how much she's worth, it's quite a lot: Millions, in fact.'

'No,' declared William: 'Her dad always kept it from her, and I promised him I'd do the same. I don't want her head bothered with financial matters. Let myself and the other trustees sort everything out.'

'You're taking away all her power,' argued Mr Ledger.

'I know my wife,' countered William, in a threatening tone.

Izzie had heard enough. No wonder Bea was bored and depressed, often bitter and taking tranquillisers.

One day Bea said, 'Izzie, I envy you your courage. I wish I'd had the spirit to stand up for myself when I was younger. It's too late for me, I've lost my chance. I'm sorry I'm sometimes nasty, but I'm angry with myself and take it out on others.'

The next day she was back to the snide remarks.

'All your wife wants to do is go shopping and drink champagne,' she said to Crispin who told Izzie about it on the drive back to London.

'What a cheek! When we stay the night, your mum opens a bottle of warm bubbly at eleven the next morning and offers me a glass, which I usually refuse. It's revolting, like mouldy, smelly cheese. It never sees the inside of a fridge. She sometimes drinks an entire bottle before lunch.' The injustice annoyed Izzie.

'That's why I told you. It's mad, but it suits Dad to keep her tipsy, he likes to be in the driving seat.'

What the heck is wrong with some rich people, thought Izzie. All those chances blighted by greed and the need to control. Crispin's mum was so bored she didn't know what to do with herself, and any confidence she may have enjoyed in the past had faded with her once gorgeous looks.

Izzie and her mother-in-law sometimes ambled over the fields behind the house. The strolls were often successful, the fresh air and scenery lifting Bea's spirits a little.

Arriving back from a restaurant lunch, to celebrate Bea's birthday, Izzie said, 'How about our walk? I could do with the exercise to work off the two helpings of cake.'

'I've never seen a girl eat like you. You'll get fat if you're not careful and my son will be off with someone else. I can't come for a walk: I'm sixty now and too old for that sort of thing. The doctor said not to do anything too strenuous.'

Some doctor!

Izzie never got her mother-in-law out across the fields again, and Bea sat in her chair most days, gazing out of the window, or at the television. Usually, after supper and a few glasses of wine, she retired to bed early.

ONE FINE SPRING DAY as they were in Crispin's white convertible Aston Martin DB6, driving to visit his parents, Izzie remarked on some cute lambs skipping around a field.

'I'm going to buy one for Mother, cheer her up. She loves animals. I can see the farmer over there.'

'Don't be daft, Crispin. You can't march onto a farm and purchase a lamb. It's not like buying a goldfish.'

He stopped the car and got out. 'Watch me.'

Izzie sat both horrified and amused as he spoke to the farmer who shook his head. Then Crispin pulled out a wad of notes, peeling a few off and giving them to the bemused man, who continued with the head shaking.

Crispin peeled more notes from the wad.

The farmer nodded.

Minutes later Crispin handed a lamb through the open roof of the car. 'Pop it on your knee, Izzie.'

'Your mum will go mad. And how come you had all that cash with you?'

'She'll love it.' Crispin ignored the question about money. He turned on his Beach Boys CD, revved the powerful engine, and they were off. 'What shall we call the lamb?'

'Larry.'

'I Get Around' blared from the speakers as the car sped away - the lamb certainly was getting about.

Crispin's parents were furious and gifted poor Larry to a local farmer.

ONE OF IZZIE'S DREAMS had been to have more free time to be a bookworm. The reality was an anticlimax. It had been the bliss of finding time to read from within a busy schedule that was a hedonistic treat. She felt guilty reading in the day and thought she should do something productive.

IN A BLINK, FOUR YEARS passed since marrying Crispin and, to her surprise and annoyance, Izzie wasn't content. She'd thought once there were no money worries; life would be perfect. It wasn't. The novelty of the social whirl and travel wore off, and reality stared her in the face. And there was a secret she was trying to battle.

Izzie had become anxious again and planned to visit a therapist in Wimbledon, Anne Clerridge, recommended by her GP.

'There is something wrong with me,' she confessed during her first visit. 'I have everything I ever wanted, but I'm not happy.'

'Have you got everything, what do you want from life, Izzie? Answer without thinking.'

'I don't know. Everyone keeps telling me I'm lucky, which makes me feel guilty. I must be one of the most selfish people in the world.'

A smile tugged at Anne's lips. 'You're not selfish; you have a right to feel happy, we all do. It's a cliché, I know, but money doesn't buy happiness. My first husband was rich, and just like you, I felt guilty about feeling miserable. Most of my friends were jealous of the large house and grounds. My mum thought I'd hit the jackpot, so it felt churlish to complain. One day I looked at my beloved spouse and wished he was dead, and then had fantasies about how nice it would be if he died.'

'But you didn't kill him?' said Izzie, with a grin.

'No, but some nights when I listened to him snoring beside me, I imagined stabbing him. That's when I knew I needed to get out. But he chipped away at my confidence over the years, and it blighted my courage, so I visited a therapist, who gave me the courage to ask for a divorce.'

'And were you happier after that?' asked Izzie.

'Very much so, I'm not telling you this to encourage you to get divorced or to murder Crispin, but to let you know I wasn't happy with my wealthy husband either, and there is no need to feel guilty. Whether we are happy with someone or not has little to do with money.'

'But surely it's better to be with the wrong person and rich, rather with the wrong person and poor?'

'It's better to be by yourself, than with the wrong person, Izzie.'

'I'm sure you're right. I'm glad you told me about your husband; it makes me feel much better. But maybe I've got too much time on my hands and should get a job? Crispin doesn't want me to, as we wouldn't be able to go away at a moment's notice. He's a structural engineer, working for the family company and can almost take time off whenever he wants.'

'Do you want to get a job?'

'No.'

'Why, Izzie? I'm not being judgmental, just curious.'

'I should sort myself out, while I don't have to work. Having time to myself is a luxury I should make the most of: I don't want these worries to get worse. They're drowning me. When I was with my first husband, I always stepped around him, trying to keep the peace, and it was the same with Mum. I've realised I don't know who I am. I know I sound spoilt, but the despair is dark and terrifying. Scary thoughts and anxieties are dominating me. Did you feel like that?'

'Yes, carry on, Izzie.'

'I'm like a shell, everyone including Crispin has been telling me what I should think and feel, where we should go on holiday, what clothes to wear, and blah de blah. It's taken such a hold that at the moment I couldn't even tell you what my favourite colour is or whether I prefer hot or cold weather, crisps or chocolate.'

'Oh, come on, surely that's an exaggeration. If I offered you a bar of chocolate or a packet of crisps right now, which would you have.'

'Both!'

Anne chuckled. 'And what about a choice of a holiday on the ski slopes or the beach?'

'Oh, beach, I'm about as good at skiing as I am at scuba diving!'

'There you go,' said Anne. 'You haven't lost your mind; you know what you want.'

'I suppose, but I do feel like a pathetic mouse, acting like a happy lioness on the outside while feeling timid inside. I'm turning into my mother. People don't realise I feel like this on the inside because I'm outgoing, with a cheerful facade.'

'So you don't want to be a timid mouse, Izzie?'

'Squeak, squeak. No, I do not! I want to be a firecracker.'

'Then a firecracker you will be. Shall we make you another appointment?'

'Yes, please.'

AFTER SEEING ANNE FOR a while, Izzie was enjoying life more and seeing things with greater clarity. She also realised how much others manipulated her, and where much of her anxiety originated. Rose was unpredictable and volatile when Izzie was growing up, and she never knew when her mum would fly into a rage or go into a sulk. One day she would be tolerant when Izzie was quite naughty, and the next go berserk over something minor.

Aged eight, when Izzie was singing 'Sunny Afternoon' by The Kinks, which alludes to a 'big fat mama', Rose went berserk: 'What did you say? What did you say? Get up to your room, and I'll deal with you later.' And on another day, she'd have laughed and sung along.

Rose was often riddled with anxiety, and it rubbed off on Izzie. 'Oh, I can't wait to go on holiday this year. Are you looking forward to it, Mum?' Izzie enthused, back in 1965.

'All being well, we'll be going on holiday. Don't tempt fate.'

'What do you mean all being well? You told me you and Dad booked it last week.'

'Yes, but you never know, something terrible could happen which could stop us going.'

Instead of feeling excited Izzie was worried. It was the sum of many incidents like this which made her anxious for the future. She was annoyed at first when she realised how much her mum had affected her, but Anne said Rose always did the best she could at the time and must have learned this behaviour from someone. Izzie knew who this was.

IZZIE'S MUM'S MOTHER died of tuberculosis when Rose was only four, and she was then brought up by her grandma, Izzie's great grandma, known as Ma. They all lived in the same street as Ma until the move over the water, when she stayed behind in Liverpool. Although she was a big-hearted old woman, she drove Izzie mad with her fussing and worrying.

Ma would go to the front door and shout all Izzie's little friends to come over, saying things like, 'Make sure she doesn't leave the street,' even to children younger than Izzie, who was furious.

'Tell me about it,' Rose said when Izzie was reminiscing years later. 'She was an even bigger worrier than me, which is saying something. Until I got married, Ma wouldn't rest until I was home from school, and later on work, or an evening out. She was even worse on dark winter nights when she would sit on the doorstep waiting. Every time she heard footsteps, she'd shout, *is that you, Rose? Is that you?* You can imagine how many times she called out to the wrong person. I felt sorry for her, but it was hard to enjoy a night out knowing she'd be worried sick, and getting cold out on the doorstep. Apart from anything else it was embarrassing.'

Izzie has fond memories of Ma despite the constraints on her freedom. The old lady was kind with a good sense of humour.

When Ma was waiting for a cataract operation, Izzie and her big brother played a trick. They found a pair of glasses without lenses and told her to try them as they'd had them made specially. 'Oh, yes. I can see much better through these,' she said.

Of course, she was maybe playing a trick on *them*.

Ma could also be funny, unintentionally. One evening she accompanied them all to the pictures, to see Norman Wisdom in *The Bulldog Breed* at the Rialto. In the old cinemas, the seats would flip up, like London taxi seats, to make it easier to move along the rows. Ten minutes into the film Rose asked if Ma was enjoying it.

'Oh, yes, but the chair is uncomfortable.'

Ma was sitting on the edge of her seat and hadn't put it down.

Another time she said, 'Have you given the budgie his thrill?'

'Don't you mean Trill?'

In 1965 Ma went to Sefton General Hospital for her cataract operation. Izzie went to visit, with her mum but was terrified of the strict sister, who made her wait in an austere disinfectant-scented corridor, not willing to flout the strict rule that disallowed children to visit patients. A brave nurse took Izzie by the hand to the outside of the hospital where she was allowed to wave at Ma, through the window, standing on a chair.

Afterwards, the kindly soul gave Izzie a glass of vile-tasting warm orange squash in a green plastic cup, with an arrowroot biscuit. *Yummy* - the snack made Izzie feel sick, but she forced it down, not wanting to upset the nurse.

Although it didn't seem much at the time, years later Rose told her how thrilled Ma had been when Izzie waved through the window.

AFTER OFFLOADING AND reminiscing to Anne one day Izzie said, 'I feel mean moaning about people like Mum and Ma, as, in the main, their intentions were good, as you say, although Mum was super-scary when angry. But I know their attitudes have contributed to my worries, expecting things to go wrong all the time. I hate this state of high anxiety over trivia. It's ridiculous. Whenever my mother couldn't locate her purse, she was hysterical until it she found it: This happened nearly every day, but she never actually lost it.'

'We're in for the long haul today,' said Anne. 'Fancy a coffee and flapjacks?'

'Yummy.'

As Anne pottered in the kitchen, Izzie thought back to a typical incident of the missing purse variety.

'Oh, God, my purse, my purse, what have I done with it, Izzie?'

'I just watched you put it back in your handbag.'

'Oh, did I? I thought I might have left it in the shop.'

'Mum, why don't you check your bag before going into a major panic?'

With fumbling shaking hands Rose unzipped her bag. Izzie watched her sag with relief.

'Oh, yes, there it is. Thank goodness. What a terrible moment.' Rose's face broke into a broad smile, and she skipped along the road, celebrating the re-acquaintance with her precious purse - until the next time.

Anne came back in with a tray of goodies. 'Carry on, Izzie. And be careful of your drink. It's extra-hot.'

Izzie took a sip of coffee, burning her tongue, and returned to her spiel: 'It drove us all crazy because we got pulled into the high drama over nothing, almost on a daily basis. However, I feel I should now list all Mum and Ma's good points to counteract the negativity.

'Luckily, Dad was relaxed and laid-back. He told me that after what he saw in the war, every day was a bonus and to be enjoyed and appreciated. Thank God for Stan. Imagine if I'd had two anxious parents! But I know Mum's anxiety drove him mad, as well.'

Anne assured her she was far from alone. 'Many people who come to see me do so because they feel guilty for not feeling the way they should about a parent, or whoever. Realising they're not alone makes them feel better. Plus, if you went to the doctor with a sore arm, you wouldn't show him the one that was perfectly well, would you? How can we make you happier, if you don't discuss what's bothering you?'

'That makes me feel better.' said Izzie.

And it did.

The last of the family diamonds

WITH ANNE'S HELP, IZZIE realised she and Crispin were not right for each other. It was time to move on - again. Drat! She'd wanted to settle into a comfortable and cosy, not to mention luxurious, married life, but her subconscious was having none of it. Whenever she lied to herself, the anxiety monster paid an unwelcome visit. She was like Pinocchio, but punished with silly fears, instead of an expanding nose.

She knew her worries would sound daft to others, but they were terrifying inside her head. There was nowhere to hide from the searchlight of her inner truth - if she wasn't happy deep down, it knew - and taunted her with terrible anxieties until she did something about it.

She told Crispin she was seeing a therapist. 'Give me the phone number,' he said.

'I thought you were confident and sure of yourself, and nothing bothered you.'

'You should have tried being bundled off to boarding school at eight years old. We couldn't even go to the bog in the morning without the matron inspecting the toilet bowl to check our bowels had worked.'

Izzie grimaced. 'Yuk, gross!'

Crispin wanted to see Anne but on his own. At first, she refused, saying it was most unethical, as she already saw Izzie and the proper way to do it was if they came as a couple. However, Crispin persisted: After his wife's glowing reports he wanted Anne and only Anne. 'I'm phoning her myself,' he said.

At Izzie's next visit Anne was rueful. 'I said point blank I wouldn't see him. One phone call and he persuaded me. What a charmer.'

'I'm glad you can see what I've been up against: He's been persuading me into everything since we met. He even planned the wedding, insisting on a lavish affair, saying his mum would be upset if we had a small function, but I knew it was him who wanted the big wedding.'

Izzie told Jack about it at the time. 'I wish we could go and get married on a beach. I don't want the fuss; after all, it's my second marriage. Men aren't meant to care about this stuff.'

'He wants to be a September bride,' said Jack.

Izzie sniggered before taking another sip of Kir Royale. 'Well, I'm going to insist on a buffet and not one of those stodgy sit-down affairs.' And in that, she got her way:

After the wedding in Westminster Register Office and a blessing at St George's church, they gave a daytime barbecue reception at Kensington Roof Gardens, with pink flamingos wandering around the lawn. A string quartet played, and the sun shone.

Izzie wore a beautiful David Fielden bias-cut silk dress and enjoyed floating around and chatting with friends and family. Crispin wore a natty suit, designed by Tommy Nutter. It was a perfect day. Afterwards, they flew by helicopter to Clifton Towers, a stately home, turned hotel, about ten miles from Heathrow, ready to leave for their honeymoon in Aruba the next morning.

The evening was somewhat marred by them being too tired to eat the wonderful dinner they'd been looking forward to; Izzie nearly dropped her head into the soup, at which point they gave up and lumbered straight to their luxurious four-poster bed.

As Izzie was finally drifting off, she heard the angelic choir from St George's singing 'Love Divine all Loves Excelling'.

The next morning was great fun. Breakfast was in authentic stately home style, with all the guests eating at one large table. The other patrons were Americans over for a family party. They had Izzie in stitches, which took all the possible austerity from the occasion. It was as fun as a night in the local pub.

IZZIE WAS HALF LOOKING forward to, half dreading the honeymoon - they were going scuba diving: Crispin's choice. She preferred to be on top of the water - not under it, alternating with a sun lounger, holding a novel in one hand and a cold drink in the other, and the occasional relaxing swim to cool off.

And it *was* a scuba-diving honeymoon, not a honeymoon with a little scuba-diving. Most residents in the hotel went on three dives a day; morning, afternoon and night: It reminded Izzie of Honey's dating schedule.

All anyone talked about was diving. Izzie thought she would go mad after day two. They had to be at breakfast at eight every morning, ready to leave on the first dive of the day at nine. There was a sign on a blackboard in the dining area reminding them not to overeat, or drink any alcohol before a dive. When on earth were they meant to enjoy themselves? It was always before a flipping dive. Izzie had to accompany Crispin, or he wouldn't have had a dive buddy, which was against the safety rules, no matter how many others were enjoying the underwater delights at the same time.

Izzie reluctantly agreed to the morning and afternoon dives, but flatly refused the evening variety, because of pure terror. Crispin persisted: 'It isn't fair; I can't go on the night dives unless you come.'

'Not fair? A scuba diving holiday would never be my choice in a million zillion years. I'd have been happy with a weekend in Paris. I already spent our holiday in Barbados last year doing a dive course so we could make this trip.

'At first, I thought, wow, Barbados, I'm lucky - until I found out you'd booked me into an intense scuba qualification regime. I was in scuba school morning and afternoon, every day for two weeks, with the final exam on Christmas Day.'

'Luxury,' joked Crispin.

'Ha! I had one afternoon off in two weeks and told you I wanted to relax on the beach with my book. After ten minutes you came over and asked if I'd finished relaxing as you wanted to go into town, to buy some new flippers.'

'And a fine pair of flippers they are, too, Izzie.'

'On Christmas Day, straight after an early breakfast, I was answering questions about the bends, equalisers and other endless scuba diving related paraphernalia, equipment and rules. That was only the theory test. Then I was only allowed a small lunch because I had the practical test on Christmas afternoon. So when I would normally be watching The Queen's speech, recovering from turkey overload, I was proving I could take all my equipment off, including mask and breathing apparatus while sitting underneath fifteen feet of water.'

'But, you must admit it was jolly funny when you took your bikini top off, along with your buoyancy compensator,' said Crispin, chuckling. 'I believe the look on everyone's face was priceless. I'm so glad your instructor told me about it.'

One of the lovely things about Crispin was his almost permanent good nature.

'I'm glad you were amused,' said Izzie, starting to laugh. 'Oh, OK, I'll come on a night dive, as long as you promise that if I hate it, you won't pressure me again. And can we do something else, apart from diving, at least one day while we're here?'

'Done.' said Crispin. 'You choose, as long it involves hiring a 4x4.'

Not the ideal answer, which would have been, 'Let's spend the day languishing on the beach, darling.' But it was better than diving.

THE NIGHT DIVE WAS one of the worst experiences of Izzie's life. When they said 'night', they weren't lying. It was pitch-black. They were all issued with underwater torches and told to stay close to the instructor. Izzie was terrified as she fell back from the boat into dark aquatic depths.

About thirty feet down everyone gathered around a puffer fish, shining their lights on it. It must have felt as if it were on stage: The Maggie Smith of the underwater world.

As Izzie focused on trying to enjoy the experience, rather than wishing herself back on land, she felt excruciating pain in her ears. She'd obviously not equalised sufficiently and felt as if her eardrums would burst. She must rise through the water to relieve the pressure before popping back to join the group. And if that failed, she'd head for the safety of the lit-up dive boat.

All she could think about was getting rid of the pain. Her head felt it would detonate. She came up a little, held her nose and blew gently. Sweet relief, the agony eased a little. She could try and get back to the group. Gently descending she looked for torch lights: None, nowhere. The only thing was to get to the surface and swim to the boat.

Breaking the surface, Izzie looked for the dive vessel. It may as well have been the *Mary Celeste* because she couldn't see it or any lights anywhere in any direction. She was in dark waters and was about to die. She saw the newspaper headline:

Honeymooning Woman Eaten by Shark, off Aruba.

Something grabbed Izzie's ankle. The predator sank its teeth into her flesh and was dragging her to a watery death. Intuition had told her she wasn't a natural scuba diver, but a snorkeler, at best. She should have listened. Then she saw lights - torches. The instructor had come to rescue her, accompanied by Crispin. Getting back on the boat Izzie expected her new hubby to be sympathetic.

'I can't believe you ruined that dive,' he said.

THE BEST PART OF THE honeymoon was the finale. One evening Crispin said, 'I've made a mistake. Three weeks in this place is too much, even for me. How about we bail out and go to Los Angeles for the last week?'

'Are you sure it's not because of me, spoiling things because I'm not Jane Cousteau or Aqua Marina?'

'No. It's too quiet here. I want some action. LA will be a riot.'

Off they gadded to Los Angeles. Izzie loved and adored it and was on a high for the entire week. The only fish she saw were on plates in the fabulous and lively restaurants.

'All that scuba-diving was a bit overkill, wasn't it?' said Crispin, over dinner in Santa Monica one evening.

'Just a little, but why aren't you wearing your new flippers? You could have gone for a quick dive after pudding.'

'Tee-hee.'

Izzie and Crispin experienced many wonderful times together, but in reality, and eventually, although they were great mates, they weren't quite right for each other. Izzie reckoned if you took away all the glitz, glam, holidays, social whirl, high income, posh house etc. then their relationship alone wouldn't sustain them. She imagined Crispin in a three-bedroom semi, and the image of a caged lion popped into her head.

One evening Izzie put a hypothetical situation to him: 'Crispin, would you be content if we both earned an average wage and lived in an ordinary house in the suburbs?'

'Would I still have the Bentley or Aston Martin and be able to go skiing and scuba diving?'

Izzie laughed and gave up.

Besides everything else, Crispin admitted he wanted children and Izzie couldn't visualise herself in that role. If she tried to imagine the maternal route, she almost got a panic attack. No, it wasn't for her, and it wasn't fair to either of them.

Maybe, if they got divorced, Crispin's next wife or girlfriend would be a mermaid. He'd like that.

IZZIE WAS MEETING HER husband for dinner one night, in Langton's, one of her favourite restaurants. Crispin was coming straight from work. She meant to wait until they'd had a few glasses of wine to share her feelings, but couldn't hold back as she announced, for the second time in her young life, 'We should get divorced.'

Izzie worried she'd been tactless. To her surprise, Crispin said, 'Good idea. You're not the only one with a shock announcement. I've been dreading telling you something for ages but was hoping to sort it out. One of the reasons I've been seeing Anne is because I've lost an enormous amount of money on a bad investment that's gone tits up. I'm going to have to get a proper job, no more gadding around the world. And my cars will have to go.'

'You might even have to get on a bus. You know, those big red things, with wheels.' Izzie joked but was horrified. There she was, hoping to start an exciting new life, but it wouldn't be much fun with no money. And how was Crispin going to manage, how would he cope without all the little, and large, luxuries he thought were everyday necessities? After all, not having enough money to buy white-wall tyres for his Bentley had been poverty.

'Oh, my God, what the hell are we to do?' worried Izzie. 'And why do you look so annoyingly calm?'

'We'll be OK. I have something for you,' said Crispin, procuring a leather box from his briefcase. 'I know how you worry about not having money behind you, so this should solve matters.'

Izzie opened it. Inside was a diamond ring, earrings and pendant set. The jewels were substantial, round and dazzling: Stunning, but not for her, a lover of costume jewellery. She didn't like the worry of wearing real jewels. Bea once lent her an emerald ring and had driven them both mad, ringing every night to check it was safely in the safe.

'I don't understand,' said Izzie. 'And how come you've got them with you? It's all too pat.'

'Before this conversation, I was going to suggest we sell them and live on the proceeds until we got back on our feet. But you can have them as a divorce settlement. Each diamond is at least six carats.'

'Where did you get them?'

'Remember when my parents died and we had to sell off jewellery to pay death duties?'

'Yes,' said Izzie. Crispin's mum had died two years before, followed by his dad six months later.

'Well, I managed to keep hold of these, and they're yours: The last of the family diamonds. A chap I know in Hatton Garden said the price of diamonds is set to rise in a few months. So, if I were you, I'd pop them in a deposit box for now. I've even organised one for you at Coups Bank, here are the details and the key.'

Crispin passed Izzie an envelope. 'Also, I've spoken to the manager, and he's willing to let you keep an account there, once we dissolve the joint one.'

Izzie knew she'd played into his hands. 'It's obvious you were about to ask for a divorce. Why else would you just happen to have the jewels and safe deposit key with you and have already organised my future with the bank?'

Crispin grinned. 'Guilty, as charged.'

Izzie loved being a Coups customer; it was rather fun. A doorman in top hat and tails met her at the door. And whenever she saw the manager, he offered her a sherry.

She popped the envelope and box into her bag; luckily, she had a large one with her, not some useless little evening clutch. The contrast between her two husbands was insane - Hubby the First would worry when carrying ten pounds in cash, whereas Hubby the Second moved diamonds around London as if they were a bag of dolly mixtures.

'Earth to Izzie, you're daydreaming,' said Crispin. 'In the meantime, I can manage to give you twenty grand, so you've got enough money to be going on with, rent a place to live and everything. Let's have an easy amicable divorce. OK?'

'You know me, even if it wasn't fine I couldn't be bothered contesting it. I want to get on with my life, not waste energy. Charles Dickens's *Bleak House* put me off ever getting involved in a legal wrangle. Not that I read it all - it was too much like living through it myself.'

'Trust you to refer everything back to a book.' Crispin paused. 'And there's something else, I've met someone.'

'Ha! You cunning fox: And she's rich, isn't she? I knew there must be a reason you were so calm about money and the divorce.'

'Yes, totally loaded, to be honest. I've fallen for my lawyer, Lady Loveday.'

'Oh, I read about her in Greetings! last week. She's seriously rich: You jammy bugger!'

They both laughed, and it felt good.

'I doubt your cars will have to go.' said Izzie.

'Maybe not, if I play my cards right, but it sounded rather effective, didn't it?'

'Hang on a minute. I bet the only reason you were seeing Anne was to see how the ground lay re asking for a divorce, and you didn't lose money on a bad investment.'

'How could you think such a thing, shall we have pudding?' asked Crispin.

Izzie was not in the least bit offended or upset, which told her it was the right decision. But it was a bit insulting her first husband had been equally happy to let her go.

Never mind, she was the lucky recipient of the last of the family diamonds, and twenty grand, to get her on the road to an exciting new life.

Izzie & Martha, May 1996

STEPPING INTO A CAB to take her home, after a spot of early shopping, Izzie grins at the memories. 'Grosvenor Square, please.'

As the cab trundles through town, her mind dwells on Doris. She is such a tonic, and it's a relief that although she has her own cleaning company, she still works for Izzie. The other customer Doris cleans for, Martha from Brighton, is the new client Izzie will see this morning: She must be something special, for Doris to travel to Brighton to work for her two days a week.

'Oh, I don't mind, love, and she's a darling with a heart of gold. I sometimes stay with my son, who lives in Kemptown. The drive doesn't take me too long from our house in Clapham, which is just as well, as James, her despot of a husband, demands an early start. He never got over his brief army career. It's a wonder he doesn't wake up poor Martha with a bugle call. Also, I like shopping in Barrington's Department Store, when I'm there. It reminds me of Grace Brothers.'

Doris gave Martha the final nudge she needed to see Izzie when she said, 'I'm worried you'll crack up if you don't sort yourself out soon. You're not much more than a doormat.'

Izzie's thoughts are interrupted by the cab driver: 'Nearly there, love, what number is it?'

'Drop me off here, and I'll walk. I could do with a bit of fresh air.'

Arriving at her address Izzie spots a harried looking woman who looks in about her mid to late forties, coming from the other direction. She's quite attractive, in a faded no-makeup way, with shoulder-length auburn hair, streaked with grey, held back in a velvet headband. She wears a dull grey tweed suit, with a white blouse, flat lace-up shoes, and an anxious expression.

Flipping heck, she looks like a librarian from the 1950's. I bet that's Martha.

'Are these the premises of the Second Chance Club?' asks the librarian from the past.

'You must be Martha? I'm Izzie. Let's go inside, and I'll fire up the cappuccino machine. Come on; let's get on with your new life. The office is on the top floor. When I want to be posh, I call it the penthouse.'

A few perfect cappuccinos later, and half a box of tissues to mop up flowing tears, Martha has unburdened herself.

'Why are you putting up with it all?' asks Izzie.

'It's become a habit. I want to be braver and stand up to James, but when I say anything, it's always turned around to make me into an ingrate or the guilty party. He should have been a barrister. I've become a coward.'

Izzie is reminded of Bea and feels sad. She asks, 'What makes you feel brave, or most alive?'

'When I ride my beautiful horse: James has banned me for now as he's scared I'll fall off again, soon after my last tumble and do myself permanent damage. I reckon it's because he hated it when I couldn't go to work. The office didn't run as smoothly when I was in bed for a while. Every time I try and argue about it, he goes mad, so I've backed down for now. I don't have the energy for more rows. I'm exhausted but so angry with myself for being such a wimp and letting James boss me around.'

'Couldn't you ride Arabesque when your husband is out?'

'I'm too worried he'll come home and see me. Apart from that, he organises my life like a military regime. Today I'm supposed to be seeing a physiotherapist. I told James I was having problems typing after the fall. He hates it when I can't keep up with the letters.'

'Could you find some excuse to pop up to London regularly, Martha? My idea, if it all sounds good to you, is at least one private or group session with me, and one equine adventure a week. It sounds important we find a way to get you on a horse, even if it isn't your beloved Arabesque. And you can get together with the other recruits at any time. When you feel a little more confident, we can tackle other matters and your wardrobe and image, if you like. Do you like your clothes? You're pulling and glowering at them.'

'I hate them, but you're right; my priority is to get on a horse again. Riding makes me feel alive. What do you mean about the equine adventures and who are the other recruits?'

'I usually take on no more than three clients at a time,' explains Izzie. 'You can make plans and exchange contact details in the first group session if that's what you all want. It's helpful and therapeutic to have mates who are going through similar experiences. Doris is still friends with the other two in her group. Apart from anything else, it's great fun, and not compulsory. You've had enough of being told what to do. From experience, it's super-effective. As for the equine adventures, will riding here in London suffice for now?'

'Yes, I need to ride, but I'm pathetic not standing up to my husband.'

'You are *not* pathetic. James manipulated you for a long time; it will take a little while to get control of your life again. You're allowing him to be more valuable than yourself. We are all equally important. You could ride in Hyde Park. I've got an ex-client who co-runs a riding school. I'll give you her card, mention my name and you'll get mate's rates.'

'I like the sound of this,' says Martha.

'You could stay here whenever it's tricky getting back to Brighton. This place has a granny or nanny annexe with a bathroom and tiny kitchen so we wouldn't be under each other's feet. There won't be any extra charge.'

'Wow, I'd love it. Thanks. I'll have to make up the odd white lie to let James know why I'm away and sometimes won't come home. I might have to invent an old and sick aunt. I'll christen her Aunt Agatha: If I tell James she might leave me some money in her will, he'll let me go like a shot. I always felt guilty lying to him before today, but I now feel I'm not alone, which has given me a little courage. He tells loads of lies, so he'll get a little of his own medicine, and about time. Would it be OK to keep my riding gear in the annexe?'

'Of course, I presumed you would.'

'Do you ride?' Martha asks.

'No. I rode a pony called Shamrock when I was six, at Butlin's. When I got on a horse a few years ago, I was terrified. I've left it too late to become the female Scobie Breasley.'

'Did you only ride Shamrock the once?'

'Yes. I looked forward to reacquainting myself with my trusty steed for an entire year and nagged my parents to take me riding on the first day of our holiday. When I was asked to choose my pony, I said I wanted Shamrock. "He's dead" was the reply I got from a stern looking woman.'

'Didn't she sugar coat it a little?'

'Not at all: Nothing.'

Martha looks surprised: 'Wow, fancy being so direct with a child. Were you upset?'

'I was heartbroken and mourned for a few days, refusing to get on any other pony - ever. It seems dramatic now. Anyway, this is supposed to be about you, how about it Martha, do you want to join the Second Chance Club?'

'I do, but how much will it cost?'

When Izzie names a price, Martha wants to cry with relief. 'Phew, less than I thought: It all sounds too good to be true.'

'That's a cliché spouted by people who don't believe in miracles, and I know, I used to be one of them, despite reading *Pollyanna* a few times when I was a kid.'

Martha smiles: 'I love *Pollyanna*. I'm certainly glad I came here. When do I meet the others and who are they?'

'I can't tell you until they are signed up. I have one local client tomorrow morning and another from Wales who I'm seeing this afternoon.'

'I feel hope, for the first time in ages, thank you,' says Martha.

Izzie & Carlotta

'WHAT A FANTASTIC OFFICE.' Carlotta admires thick grey carpets, elegant blue sofas, French antique furniture and decadent yellow and blue curtains with swags and tails.

Izzie puts drinks and a coconut cake on the coffee table. 'Make yourself comfortable and tell me about yourself and why you want to change your life. I know you said a bit about Colin Cooper when you phoned, sorry, Wolf Song. Tell me more.'

Carlotta sinks into a luxurious sofa and takes a sip of coffee, before biting into a slice of gooey cake. She wonders how to start, although she feels relaxed already. 'Oh, my God where do I begin?'

'Don't think about it, just start talking and let the words flow.'

Two hours later Carlotta has talked herself hoarse and feels a little lighter.

Izzie has hardly said a word, sensing the client's need to vent; it's tricky as she has discovered a juicy titbit about Colin Cooper, aka Wolf Song, but is waiting for the right time to reveal her knowledge. 'What do you want to happen, Carlotta?'

'I want to ask Colin to leave without feeling guilty. Better still, I'd like him to go of his own accord. Part of me is worried he'll go ballistic if I ask him to leave. After that, I'd like to get my life back. I've lost my confidence, put on weight and hate the way I look. And I wish I was a few inches taller; I stuck at five foot four when I was fifteen.'

'Gently persuading Colin to go could be arranged. And the rest is easy, apart from changing your height, which is perfect as it is. You're an attractive woman, but it's easy to let ourselves go a bit when we're not happy. You're wearing clothes which do you no favours. I guess you have a super figure hidden under that baggy sweater, a real Gina Lollabrigida. Putting it all right should be a cinch.'

'Why's that?'

Izzie sees her moment to reveal the secret: 'For starters, I've done a little research on Wolf; he's done this before.'

'Done what before?'

'He's lived off a woman while earning no money, posing as a poet.'

Carlotta is amazed. 'What on earth do you mean?'

'Colin trained as a plumber, but it doesn't suit the artistic image he has of himself. So he's pretending to be a tortured poet. The mung bean poem you mentioned is not even his.'

'Whose is it?'

'A friend of mine wrote it as a joke. Colin liked it and passed it off as his own. I know this is a *huge* coincidence but my old schoolmate, Cindy, had the misfortune to live with him before she met her husband. Colin was probably the laziest plumber ever, and not adept at it. Cindy reckons he pretended incompetence to cover up being a lazy arse.'

'I can't take this in, but carry on,' says Carlotta.

'Apparently, he dabbled in poetry after giving up plumbing for more artistic pursuits, expecting Cindy to pay the bills. And what's more, I have an idea of how to get rid of him, without you feeling the teeniest bit guilty.'

Carlotta reels with the revelations. 'Oh My God; I don't believe it. And the cheeky sod even let me pay for a man to come and fix the broken toilet flush a few weeks ago. What a coincidence your friend lived with him. How did you find out?'

'The name Colin Cooper rang a bell when you told me a bit about him on the phone. I remembered Cindy moaning about a lazy boyfriend of the same name, who I never met. I contacted her right away; she confirmed it and popped around here last night, leaving a photo. We had quite a giggle. Is this him?'

Carlotta is amazed. 'Oh, my God, it is!'

They both have to stop talking to clutch their stomachs, as they're laughing so hard.

Izzie recovers first. 'What's funnier is Cindy reckons he left her for a woman with more money: You, I believe. I know you met at Glastonbury, which correlates with the story he told Cindy.'

'Yes, we did. However, I'm hardly wealthy, but I see where you're going with this. We're going to do a con job on him, aren't we?'

'Well, I wouldn't put it that strongly, but we *could* dangle some bait. And if Colin and his ego are silly enough to fall into such a trap, then so be it.'

'It would serve him right, Izzie!'

They make an appointment for their first proper session, and Izzie asks if Carlotta will have trouble getting back to Wales after late appointments.

'Thanks, but I'll be fine. My first and only boyfriend, before Wolf, lives in Battersea and I'll stay with him. There's no romance left, but we're great friends. In fact, I'm off to meet him now for a coffee in Bacchus on the King's Road, and then we're off to the cinema.'

'What are you going to see?'

'*Leaving Las Vegas,* or *Sense and Sensibility*, we'll decide later.'

'Does Wolf know?"

'Yes. He's happy to have the TV control to himself, he likes the children's shows, although he's bound to grumble about me taking the car.'

Izzie & Portia

THE NEXT DAY, PORTIA is sitting opposite Izzie in the penthouse, glass of sparkling water in hand.

'I had a feeling you'd call. Do spill the beans as to why you turned up so soon after our meeting on the bus.'

'Well, first of all, I decided to pop into Blossoms for lunch.'

'I used to work there, what seems like a lifetime ago.'

'Oh, my God, I've been racking my brains. I used to come in with Mum. I knew I'd seen you before; your hair was longer, wilder and darker back then. I usually ordered the spaghetti Bolognese, and a glass of coke and mum smoked salmon salad and a glass of Chablis. You admired my jeans once.'

'Of course, I thought I'd seen your beautiful face before, but I thought it was when I was reading *Vogue* or something. As for my hair, I used to dye it nearly black and have it permed, but it became too much hassle. I've now accepted my straighter, lighter locks. But, I remember you with pink short punk hair, and sprayed-on ripped jeans on endless legs. Am I right?'

'Yes, oh this is amazing. Wait until I tell Mum.'

'Our reunion calls for a little glass of fizz. Want to join me?'

'Hell, yes.'

They spend a little time reminiscing about Blossoms then Portia leads into the story of arriving home to find her husband in bed with the chauffeur.

'Are you upset about it?' asks Izzie, trying to keep a straight face.

'No, I'm not, it's funny - now. I was raging at first. And I feel like an idiot.'

'It is funny, but you're certainly not an idiot. Although I've felt like a fool many times and will do again. One of our problems is taking life too seriously, and, on that note, permission to laugh about the chauffeur hat?'

Portia feels a giggle arising. 'Go ahead.'

They both fall about, and it's a good job they're wearing waterproof mascara. Recovering, Portia envisages Antoine, naked but for his hat, and loses it, which sets Izzie off again.

'I'm glad you're fun,' says Portia. 'When I saw conventional counsellors, they had serious attitudes, and I felt like I was ill, which maybe I was. But the more grave they looked, the more of a problem I thought I had. But here I feel like I'm chatting with a non-judgmental friend. I want life to be more lighthearted, not dourer. And I hate psychobabble, so I love your straightforward attitude.'

'I went to a counsellor, Anne, in Wimbledon and she started off solemn, by the book. That didn't work for me, and I came ahead in leaps and bounds when she loosened up. She even baked flapjacks for my visits. Oh, they're yummy. I could eat one now.'

'So could I. Do you still see her?'

'Yes, I do, although not much these days. I grew to adore Anne, so I still visit her every few months for a consultation on some pretence. I'm too fond of her to stop going, and it's great to get an impartial and detached viewpoint sometimes. It's a myth that therapists and counsellors don't need help from time to time. Anyway, enough about me, this is about you. What do you want from our sessions, and life in general?'

'I want to stop feeling numb. I've always been lavished with all the trappings, but feel as if I'm acting, going through the motions, since Todd's accident. It's like I'm reading from a play and have no passion. I want to wake up excited about life like I did before.'

'Tell me more about Todd,' says Izzie, softly.

AN HOUR LATER PORTIA has poured out her heart to Izzie, who says, 'And what about Fabian, are you sure you want to move on from him?'

'Yes. Let him have Antoine. I want to get my zing back and then maybe find a boyfriend who isn't gay.'

'What we will do for you first Portia if you want, is teach you to meditate.'

'I'll never be able to. I tried it a few times. I couldn't empty my mind. I couldn't concentrate. Five minutes felt like five hours.'

'It's all included in the fee, so you might as well give it a go. And you don't need to empty your mind or concentrate. It's effortless, and the time usually flies by: Shall we make an appointment for tomorrow morning? Although we won't have champagne, a clear mind is best for learning to meditate. I do have *some* professionalism. What do you think?' Izzie picks up her diary.

'I want to go ahead, so yes; please let's make an appointment for tomorrow. I'm looking forward to it.'

'And so you should be. It's the best thing in my life, like an ace up the sleeve. Since I started meditating my life flows more smoothly, and I have more bliss and fewer blips. How is eleven o'clock for you?'

'Perfect.' Portia is excited.

Izzie Firecracker, June 1996

'HOW ARE YOUR THREE latest recruits getting on?' Doris asks a few weeks later.

'Pretty well, Doris. In fact, they've arranged to meet up for dinner tonight. And later in the week, they're all coming over for a joint session.'

'Oh, I envy them.'

'Why? You've got your wonderful new life and attitude.'

'I know, my love, but there was something about setting out on my voyage of discovery. I so enjoyed the first get-together with the others. It was great to be able to say what I wanted without anyone judging, or saying I was reaching too high. My old mates laughed when I said I wanted my own cleaning business. One cheeky cow even asked why I was getting ideas above my station. Did she think I lived above Kings Cross or something? Reckon she was jealous. Still is.'

'I'm proud of you Doris.'

'I'm proud of myself. Now, I let myself in yesterday and caught up on the cleaning, so if you're free, I'd love to hear more of the story you told me the other day. We got up to where you and Crispin decided your marriage was a no-go and he gave you the last of the family diamonds and ran off with his wealthy lawyer, Lady Muck, or whatever her name is. I can't stop thinking about it. It's like a novel. I haven't even been able to focus on my vacuuming, which I usually love.'

'You're the only person I know who loves to vacuum. I hate it, so thank God I have you. OK, Doris, let's get coffees and carry on.'

CHOCOLATE SPRINKLED cappuccinos in front of them, Izzie takes up the story:

'Crispin and I started divorce proceedings, which was a doddle as everything was agreed. I popped the diamonds in the safe deposit box at Coups Bank, as suggested. There was no rush as I had twenty thousand pounds to be going on with: I didn't want to cash in the diamonds until I knew what to do with my life. I figured the jewels would only go up in value, so they were as good as investing in a property, or whatever.

'I needed to sort my head out, so I joined a retreat, Maharishi Mansion, for a year: In exchange for me paying a small fee and doing some daily chores, I was given a bed, basic meals, and taught how to meditate, do yoga asanas, and stuff.'

Doris chuckles. 'Wow, I can't imagine you living in India, or doing chores. I bet that retreat was a right flipping mess when you were there.'

'Ha ha! It was in Bedlam Bottom, Surrey, and I escaped most weekends to stay with Cindy, who moved to London before I did, and we'd hit the clubs. If Honey weren't tied up with one of her men, probably literally, she'd join us. I'm not a purist, more middle-ground. One of the Indian gurus who visited the retreat told me to enjoy 200% of life; 100% inner spiritual and 100% outer material, and not to get the idea that meditating meant going around looking pious or being a bore.'

Doris nods. 'I know a few of those buggers. Carry on, my love.'

'I put a limit on staying at the retreat for no more than a year: I was wary of becoming institutionalised. Even when I first saw *The Sound of Music*, in 1965, I worried I'd get the calling to be a nun. Just as I was about to leave Maharishi Mansion something lucky happened.'

Doris chuckles. 'It's not bloody likely, you ever becoming a nun. Go on, I'm all ears.'

'Crispin and I met a wealthy American family when we were on holiday in Anguilla the first year we were married. At the time, the daughter, Jo, a natural beauty was sixteen. Jo and I got on well; she stuck to me like glue, and I made her laugh. She was a serious lass, with the weight of the world on her shoulders.

'Anyway, as I was packing my suitcase at the retreat, I got a phone call from Jo's dad, begging me to pop over to California as she was in a bad way and he hoped I could cheer her up. He said there was a First-Class ticket waiting for me at the airport.'

'You're a jammy bugger!'

'I know, Doris: I've always believed in a little magic since reading the *Bobby Brewster* books and watching *Bewitched* as a kid. I threw a few things in a suitcase, as they do in the movies, and headed to the airport. The flight was luxurious, and I was picked up in a limo from LAX.'

'What's LAX?'

'Los Angeles Airport, Doris.'

'Ooh! Get you. Go on, love, what was the house like?'

'It was heavenly, a pink mansion on the beach in Malibu. I was excited until I saw Jo: She looked gaunt, hollow-eyed and weighed about seven stone. And she's tall.'

'What was she upset about, with all that money?'

'A mistake many of us make, Doris, assuming if you're rich, you must be happy. I fell into that trap. I've met quite a few of these rich kids who torture themselves with guilt and worry about everything in the world as if it were their fault. I know people with hardly any money can do the same, but when the mind isn't taken up with basic living problems, such as paying the rent or mortgage, it can leave room for other worries to invade. That's one of the reasons some people go to pieces when they win the lottery.'

'I don't think I'd go to pieces, but I might buy some pieces of jewellery, but carry on, love,' says Doris.

'It's not only that they feel overwhelmed by the money, take away the concern about paying the bills, and all the worries that have been queuing up for their turn to torture attack.'

'What sort of things?' asks Doris.

'Existential flotsam often, of the why am I here, what's the point and all that crap. Ironically some wealthy people never fully enjoy their dosh as they're worried about losing it all. And being rich doesn't stop anyone stressing about money. Jack wouldn't blink over the cost of cocaine and champagne but was sometimes mean about everyday items. I remember him arguing with the nice Indian man in the corner shop because he increased the price of sparkling water; at first, I thought it was a joke, but he was genuinely angry.

'Another time he went mad at me for wasting money by not switching off a light. Anyway, whatever the reason, poor Jo was in hell. I was determined to pull her out of the dumps as it was a waste of her youth,' says Izzie.

'What did you do?'

'I gradually got her to throw away most of the useless guilt, which is self-inflicted punishment and told her all my usual stuff about being here to enjoy and life is not meant to be a struggle and blah de blah. Ironically, I also made her feel a bit guilty about being miserable. I told her that when she put her attention on sad and depressing things she would create more of the same in her life and the world in general.'

Doris laughs. 'Mad, you stopped her feeling guilty by making her feel guilty about feeling guilty.'

'It *does* sound bonkers when you put it like that. But we have to out-fool our minds when they play tricks on us. I also taught Jo to meditate which she loves, and she said it helps stop her feeling overwhelmed by life. She also joined a yoga class and looks amazing these days, like a top model, and could give Cindy Crawford a run for her money.'

Doris pouts and puts a hand on her hip. 'I hope that's what you told her about me.'

'Are you imitating a teapot? Of course, I told her I dragged you from the Paris catwalks. Anyway, Jo's parents were overjoyed, and they rewarded me by helping me set up a business. It was their idea I began doing the same for others as I had for Jo. We came up with the notion of the Second Chance Club, and my new name, Izzie Firecracker, one night over pitchers of strawberry margaritas.'

'Ooh, they sound lovely,' says Doris. 'Next time I'll come without my car, and you can make me one.'

'I'll do better than that, Doris. I'll take you to my favourite Mexican restaurant, in Covent Garden, next week.'

'I'll look forward to that; will I need to wear a Sombrero?'

'Definitely, Doris, you won't be allowed in without one. Anyway, carrying on, my American friends generously loan me this penthouse for my home and office. They only use it two months a year, and when they're over here, I go and stay in their Malibu home, seeing clients they've lined up. They never let me pay any rent because they'd otherwise have to hire a caretaker, or so they say. That's why the cost of my services is comparatively reasonable; I hardly have any overheads.'

'If someone flushed you down the toilet, Izzie, you'd come up smelling of roses.'

'I have my bad days, Doris. We all do, but on the whole, I have the anxiety monster in check and life is good. Anyway, you don't do so badly yourself, Mrs Designer-Overall.'

Cake & dinner, June 1996

IZZIE CHATS TO THE trio. 'Today is all about you. We're not discussing problems, just aspirations. Pretend you are free and single, with no money issues. For the sake of the exercise, throw boyfriends and husbands out of the equation.'

'I'm happy to do that,' says Martha. 'I'd rather throw James out of the window.'

Izzie giggles. 'Anyway, describe your perfect life, not based on compromise, and we'll take it from there. Tell me what you do for fun, for work, your dress style. You get the idea. Don't think it through; let the words come up from your subconscious. Don't be serious; it's only a game. Let loose and have fun.'

Carlotta says, 'When you say no money worries do you mean we're rich?'

'You're whatever you want to be. It's hypothetical. Who wants to start?'

Martha does. 'I don't have to stop and think. I know what I want, except some of the details are a little blurred. I work on a ranch, somewhere in the States. I'm not sure if I'm the owner or an employee. I don't care; I just want to be with horses. Every morning I hop out of bed and put on jeans and cowboy boots. I ride in a Stetson, not a riding helmet. I am fearless.

'A few times a week I meet up with friends for dinner, and we have lots of laughs over steak and red wine, or pizza and beer, drunk straight from the bottle.'

'What do you wear when you go for dinner? Are you still in the jeans and cowboy boots?' asks Carlotta.

'Probably, but not the same ones I've worn all day, I don't go out smelling of horse sweat, much as I love the aroma. Who knows, maybe I throw on a dress, not chosen by James. And I wear it with cowboy boots.'

'Yee-ha!' shouts Izzie. 'What about you, Portia?'

Portia groans. 'Oh, I knew it would be me, next. Well, I don't go back to advertising, even if they'd have me. I work in fashion and go on lots of buying trips overseas. I dress like a rock-chick again, and I've got my zing back. I no longer put my hair in a bun or chignon but wear it loose. I give all my staid and stuffy outfits to charity. I'm rich.'

'What do you spend your money on?' asks Martha.

'I splash out on clothes, excellent restaurants and holidays. I don't get money on a silver platter, well not all of it, anyway. I work damn hard and feel good about myself at the end of each day. Anyway, that's enough about me, over to Carlotta.'

Carlotta puts her head in her hands and groans. 'Oh, I don't know. I'm stuck. I'd quite like money handed to me on a silver platter or even a golden one. I can't do this, which is stupid because I'm supposed to be the creative one, the writer.'

Izzie says, 'Let the words flow. Nobody's going to hold you to it if you say one thing and do something entirely different.'

'OK, here goes. I still live in Granny's house, and I'm a partner with Nerys in the Crempog. Oh, God, I have no idea where that idea came from, my subconscious, I suppose. I'm on a roll here, excuse the cafe pun: I love the Crempog and always feel happy when I'm in there. Nerys gets stressed about it though. She keeps complaining about the chefs. Three have got in huffs and left in the last year. One of them threw a knife at the wall. The last one flounced out during a busy lunchtime. Luckily I was there and mucked in.'

'What about your writing, Carlotta, have you given it up?' asks Izzie.

Carlotta claps a hand to her mouth. 'Oh, that's telling, isn't it? I didn't consider the writing. The truth is I don't like doing the column; I hate deadlines, they take the fun away. I want to work in the cafe and write a novel for fun, with no pressure. I love baking: I might ask Nerys what she thinks. As for clothes, I wear exactly what I damn well like, whatever my weight. I reveal my inner hippie and let my hair be its wild self, without straightening it all the time. Bring on the mirrored skirts.'

'Sounds brilliant,' says Portia. 'I love it, but your weight is hardly a problem, is it?'

'I don't suppose it is. For ages, I've been trying to lose the infamous last ten pounds. I don't give a fig anymore. I intend to flaunt my curves, not hide them. This pretending lark works.'

'Talking about food makes me peckish. Who wants to go to Patisserie Valkyrie, to continue our chat?' asks Izzie.

Everyone does.

THEY'RE LUCKY TO GET a table as the place is mobbed and buzzes with chatter. Izzie chooses her favourite vanilla mille-feuille, Carlotta tiramisu, and Portia a caramel éclair.

Martha doesn't order anything, apart from Darjeeling. They ask how she can resist.

'I've lost control of everything else. I swore I'd never lose my figure again.'

Portia's mouth waters in anticipation. 'Oh, look, here's the waiter with our yummy goodies.'

Moments later Izzie swallows a succulent mouthful of pastry. 'Surely an occasional treat won't harm, Martha, have you got a sweet tooth?'

'Are you kidding? You should have seen me when I got back from finishing school. I'd eaten so many cakes and pastries I looked like I'd been blown up with a bicycle pump. Mum went crazy, she worships at Temple Skinny.'

Izzie laughs and pushes her plate across to Martha. 'Go, on, I know I'm a naughty temptress. Have a little bite, doctor's orders; you'll soon burn it off, working on that ranch.'

'My perfect life, cake *and* horses,' says Martha, popping a piece of mille-feuille into her mouth. She closes her eyes and makes sensual, X-rated noises as she chews, reminiscent of the fake orgasm scene in *When Harry Met Sally*. 'Oh, my God, I have died and gone to heaven.' A waiter walks by, and she gently touches his arm. 'Excuse me; can you bring me a portion of whatever you call this? I call it a custard slice.'

A FEW DAYS LATER THE trio is having dinner in Langton's, after getting ready at the Second Chance Club, where Martha is spending the night. They have been shown to their table and are perusing the menu, after enjoying good cold champagne at the bar.

The atmosphere buzzes. The girls are excited and have put their worries aside to take it all in. Izzie was right; it *is* a fun place.

A wealthy Scottish Laird, Jock Langton, co-owns it with Diane Dare, the busty actress who played the temptress in countless movies of the 50's and 60's. The day they offered her a role as the ingénue's grandmother was the day she retired from the acting profession and invested her money in restaurants, knowing her name, and cleavage would be a pull. Everyone said she was mad to join forces with Philip Langton; he often gets drunk and insults people.

Diane was canny and guessed Langton would be a draw rather than a repellent. She was right. People deliberately book tables, hoping to be insulted by the drunken Scotsman.

The first night Izzie visited, with Jack and another two couples, Philip reeled over to their table, looked her in the eye and said, 'Get yer tits oot, lassie,' before falling flat on the floor.

'I believe that was a compliment, don't you?' said Jack.

Izzie couldn't answer for laughing.

THE GIRLS ARE AT THEIR best tonight. Portia looks like a beautiful blonde from a Hitchcock movie, in a perfect little black dress, trimmed with white ostrich feathers, by Renaldo Ripoff, dramatised by a bold blue-red lipstick.

Martha wears brown designer jeans and cowboy boots with a coral silk shirt and matching lipstick.

Izzie took them shopping on the King's Road yesterday. The boots are from Happy Soles and the shirt from Whistler. Izzie assured Martha the coral would do wonders for her auburn hair and warm colouring. It does: 'I'm so glad I've got rid of the grey bits and had my hair layered. I don't feel depressed when I see myself in a mirror.'

The others say she looks incredible, and it's true.

Carlotta has ditched her over-tight jeans and baggy tops for a deep pink hippie style maxi dress from Spirit, which flatters her curves, worn with floral lace-up boots, by Doctor Martina. She is also rocking dramatic purple eyeliner and vibrant fuchsia lipstick.

'I'm going to have the spinach soufflé to start,' says Portia. 'It comes with anchovy sauce. Then, for the main, I'll have fish and chips.'

'Anything but lentils with a pile of overcooked veggies is good for me,' says Carlotta. 'What about you, Martha?'

'I'm starving after the riding today. Smoked salmon followed by the chicken for me. And wine, gallons of it. Oh, it's such a joy to be out and about and not stuck at home discussing stuffy business in a cold dining room, watching James shovel spotted dick into his fat face. Having to tell so many fibs to be here is so worth it. My darling husband thinks I'm visiting a sick friend. It's not a lie, Izzie was hung-over today from too much vodka in that new Russian restaurant in Fulham, the Hungry Tsar.'

They place their order, and the wine soon arrives, Sauvignon Blanc and Merlot, the latter because Carlotta has decided on steak. 'I'm having it because I'm craving protein like crazy and because part of me wants to wind Wolf up; he'd be horrified, not that I'd dare tell him. It's like being watched by the Gestapo.'

'You'd better be careful, the waiter could be a spy, employed by Wolf,' says Portia.

'It wouldn't surprise me. I've been a fool, but he creates such an atmosphere, it feels as if I may be taken out and shot if found guilty of eating a prohibited item. And I hate moodiness. I can't believe Cindy lived with my darling boyfriend. Izzie has an idea to get him to leave. I can only imagine.'

'I'm one to talk,' says Martha, 'but why don't you ask him to go? It's not as if you're married.'

'It's not that simple or doesn't seem so. I talked it through with Izzie today, and she said that sometimes when people aren't emotionally trapped, they believe it's only big things that are obstacles. However, when you are in the situation yourself, you can feel ensnared, with an impenetrable wall around you, even when others think you should and could walk away.'

'I know that feeling all too well,' agrees Martha.

'You and me both, I'm more scared of Colin than I realised. He's volatile, and I'm worried he'll blow a fuse if I ask him to go. No, it has to be of his own accord, with a bit of help from Izzie's idea, hopefully.'

Martha says, 'It's like having invisible prison bars, but at least I've felt more hopeful and confident lately. The riding today was phenomenal. I feel reborn, and a lot calmer and inwardly happy since learning the meditation. It's as if a veil has lifted and I can see more clearly. I know I want to leave James, but I haven't got the courage - yet. I dread what we'll do about dividing the money. Well, I know how he'll *want* to split it, 99% to him and 1% to me. If you decide to go it alone Portia, what will you do about money? Will it be amicable?'

'Until recently I didn't give a damn as I had an embarrassingly large inheritance, doled out monthly from Mum and Dad, but they lost a lot of money recently on some gold mine or other, and my allowance has gone down to peanuts.'

'We need more wine to carry on this discussion.' Carlotta drains her glass.

Martha gives the thumbs up. 'Great idea, bring it on. Hey, have you any idea what the evening meeting on Friday is all about?'

Portia shrugs. 'No idea. Izzie said we're all invited to a campfire ceremony and told me to vote on a choice between a wimps version, indoors, by a fireplace, or Girl Guide style, outside. I voted for indoors. She's phoning me with the venue the day before. What did you both opt for, although I probably already know?'

'Outside,' say the other two, in unison.

Portia pulls a face. 'Bugger, I'd better bring Granny's old mink coat, the weather has been rubbish.'

The trio arrives home

AT NINE O'CLOCK, THE morning after the night before, Martha reluctantly hails a cab to Victoria to catch the train to Brighton. With the effects of last night's alcohol, she's lost much of her resolve and dreads facing James. *I won't think about it now*, she resolves, Scarlett O'Hara style. Lulled by the rhythmic noise of the train she settles down for a lovely snooze.

Moments later she's in the middle of an earthquake. 'Help, we're all going to die!'

'You were asleep love.' Martha opens her eyes to see a chuckling ticket collector who announces, 'We're in Brighton.'

Oh, no: Time to face the music.

Chugging up the drive, about fifteen minutes later, Martha spots James dancing with rage on the doorstep. John Travolta, eat your heart out. As she creaks open the driver's door, he greets her. 'Where in the name of blazes have you been? We've got a meeting in town.'

'I told you I wouldn't be home until about eleven.'

'You said seven.'

'Don't be silly, that's the time I had to get up. Did you expect me to get the milk train?'

James looks furious, and Martha realises, with a jolt of pride, that her response would previously have been a *sorry, dear*. So things *are* looking up.

'And why in hell's name are you wearing jeans and cowboy boots? You look ridiculous. Do you think you're on a bloody ranch?'

'I wish,' mutters Martha. 'I'll get changed, be ready in ten.' One battle at a time; don't want him to have apoplexy. Then, maybe that might be good, save her a lot of hassle if it was fatal.

'And, what's happened to your hair? It looks a brighter red. You look like a tart,' shouts James as she heads upstairs.

She doesn't answer.

LATER THE SAME DAY, Carlotta arrives back at Nirvana Lodge. When she gets rid of Wolf, the house can go back to its traditional name of Bluebell Cottage. Opening the living room door, a pungent sickly sweet smell of marijuana assaults her nostrils. Wolf is lounging on the sofa, eating cheese and onion crisps and listening to Pink Floyd singing 'Wish You Were Here', at a deafening level. 'Wish you weren't here,' she whispers, moving across the room to turn down the music.

'Hey, I was listening to that,' says the outraged Wolf.

'How about, welcome back did you have a lovely time, darling?'

'Well, *I* certainly didn't. What am I meant to do when you take the car? I'm stuck here without transport. It's not fair.'

'I didn't know the buses and trains were on strike.'

'Of course they're not,' he snaps, 'but it's selfish of you to go off in our car with no thought for anyone else.'

'It's mine, not ours; so selfish to go off in *my* car, which I pay tax and insurance on and fill with petrol.'

'Well, you didn't pay for it; your dad gave it to you.'

'I paid him, not a fortune because it's not exactly new.' *But more reliable than you.*

'You could never live on a commune, with such an attitude.'

Carlotta grimaces. 'I can't imagine anything worse. Have you written any poetry today?'

'No. You haven't been working, so why should I?'

Another nail in his coffin. He has to go. Carlotta imagines a Wolf-free existence.

'What are you grinning at?'

'Nothing, Wolfy dear, I'm glad to be home. I missed you.'

Wolf puffs up like a peacock.

MEANWHILE, IN CLOVER Mews, Portia is sitting at the kitchen table and chatting to Fabian. Antoine has gone to visit his mum in Brixton so is well out of the way.

'I thought his mum was French,' says Portia. 'How long has she lived over here?'

Fabian looks rueful. 'Antoine's real name is Anthony; he cultivated the French accent to make himself sound sexy. It was relatively easy for him as French was his best subject at school. He's practically fluent.'

'How did you find out?' asks Portia.

'I heard him on the phone one day when he didn't know I was around, and he spoke in broad Brummie.'

'Weren't you annoyed?'

'A little, but he has other charms.'

Portia recalls the 'stamp album'. 'Let's not get into that. Anyway, enough about your phoney French boyfriend, what are we going to do?'

'I'm sorry about all this, but I wonder if we can stay married and have separate lives. My parents don't know I'm gay.'

'Neither did I until the incident. Did you find out after we married, or did I turn you off women because I'm rubbish in bed?'

'Don't be daft,' says Fabian.

'Then why?'

'You'll won't like it.'

'Try me.'

'Mum and Dad found me in an embarrassing situation when I was seventeen. Do you remember me saying how upset I was when the headmaster, Mr Striker, upped and left?'

'Vaguely.'

'Well, he was sacked. It was hushed up as it would have given the school a bad name. We were found in bed together.'

'What, in the school?'

'No, my parent's bedroom: They were away and came home early,' says Fabian.

'Oh, my God, I hope he wasn't wearing a chauffeur's hat.'

'No, but he *was* wearing his gown and mortar and caning my bare backside.'

Portia can't hold in the giggles, neither can Fabian; they're hysterical, tears pouring down their faces.

Between shrieks, Fabian says, 'Oh bloody hell, and what's more, my parents might stop my allowance and throw me out of this house if we don't stay married.'

Portia stops laughing. 'What *are* you talking about?'

'If I didn't marry by the time I was thirty, and stay married for the foreseeable, they threatened to cut me off; they were sick of me gadding about and wanted me to settle down with a nice girl. I never admitted I was gay and said I was bi. To be honest, I wanted it to be true, for an easier life.'

'You bastard, you only married me to avoid being cut off?'

'Well, not only that. You were and *are* bloody gorgeous. I was, and *am*, proud to be seen with you. I'm sorry it hasn't worked out. But I'm not bi, that's for sure.'

'Do you think they *would* cut you off?' asks Portia, thinking about what she'd like to cut off.

'Well, hopefully not. Somehow, I don't care as much since the Antoine incident. I've been scared of the truth coming out. The reality isn't as bad as my anxiety-ridden imaginings.'

'It wasn't only the truth that came out,' says Portia.

Fabian blushes. 'No, it certainly wasn't. Maybe we should get divorced?'

'I can't see any option, and if they do cut you off at least you have this house, maybe you can spare me a few bricks.'

'Ah, there's a snag there. We need to talk, and it needs wine. You get the glasses, and I'll get the vino.'

SITTING ON ONE OF THE floral sofas, Fabian says, 'With my new bravery, I went to see Mum and told her everything. I thought she'd be furious, but she burst into tears and said she had no room to talk, as she's being blackmailed.'

Portia's mother-in-law is attractive, rather prim, but never unpleasant. 'Who would have anything on your strait-laced mum?'

'As you know, she owns most of Sloane's Department Store. The general manager, Sidney Snape is blackmailing her, but she won't say what about. Apparently, the fact she's Managing Director has become irrelevant; she's just a pawn in his nasty game. Since Snape took over, the business has been doing badly, and profits have slumped horribly.

'Sidney the Snake seems to be deliberately sabotaging the place. Mum wants to be rid, but if she sacks him, he's promised a most unsavoury article will appear in the papers. Recently he's also demanded extra cash payments, on top of his inflated salary.'

Portia is aghast. 'What on earth could he be blackmailing her about?'

'Mum doesn't want to say unless it becomes entirely necessary. But she does have an answer to our problems if we can solve hers. If I can get rid of Snape, without hiring a hit-man, she's promised me 49% of Sloane's. She'd planned to gift me the shares in a few years anyway. If that happens, she wants me to assist in building profits back up.

'If you help me successfully oust Sidney, I'll transfer 10% to you, to make amends. And you could then help us make the shop profitable and fabulous again. Are you in?'

'Definitely, but what's that got to do with the house?'

'It's in Mum's name, and she's worried she'll have to sell it to cover the loss of profits and the blackmail money. Dad doesn't know.'

'Shit.'

The fire ceremony

'HEY, I THOUGHT THIS was supposed to be the Girl Guide version of a campfire,' says Martha. 'I'd like to know how many of them have campfires in the lush gardens of fabulous homes beside the River Thames, in Richmond. This reminds me of that movie; *Troop Beverly Hills*, with Shelly Long. She plays the socialite, Phyllis, who takes her daughter's Wilderness Girls group on camping trips - to a posh hotel!'

'Sound like my sort of thing,' says Portia. 'Todd was into camping, and I said I'd go with him, as long as we pitched the tent in a suite at the Glitz.'

Izzie laughs. 'The reason we're here is that a mate is on holiday and begged me to come and water the plants, which are more like triffids: When I told her about the ceremony, she insisted we have it here.'

'If we were in my garden, we'd be a few feet from the neighbours and in danger of getting soot over someone's washing,' says Carlotta.

They're sitting in comfortable lounging chairs, on a stylish patio, next to a large fire pit. In case the weather turns chilly, there are outside heaters dotted around. An appetising aroma wafts from a wood-burning barbecue as sausages and burgers brown to perfection.

'We'll enjoy these then get down to business. And I'm a lazy arse, so it's paper plates; no washing up. I suggest no alcohol until after the ceremony; it's best your heads are clear. Afterwards, we can break open the bubbly,' says Izzie.

Martha has knife and fork at the ready. 'Are those sausages cooked? Eating outdoors makes me ravenous.'

Portia grins. 'When I was having dinner with Fabian one evening, the meal took ages to arrive, and I said I was ravishing. He said he agreed, but didn't I mean ravenous?'

'You always look ravishing, it's not fair,' says Martha.

'Sausages coming up!' shouts Izzie.

The girls tuck into the feast. Before pudding and fizz, Izzie hands out pens and notepads. 'Right, you've been meditating for a while and hopefully feeling better and less stressed. Meditation is often enough for most pressures to leave on their own, enabling us to think with more clarity. It's similar to coming off caffeine when you've been a coffee junky, like me.

'Our new heightened awareness often means that therapy and counselling work better and faster to pinpoint what's stressing or holding us back. Often it's things that happened when we were young which stay to haunt us, robbing us of inner peace.'

'What like?' asks Portia.

'I have a perfect example, which a client, Jeremy, said I could pass on: He was in a dreadful state when he came to see me, and considering suicide due to a hideous thing he did when younger. He'd become overly-accommodating to everyone to compensate for his evil ways.'

Carlotta pauses, mid burger-bite. 'Blimey, did he commit armed robbery or something?'

'It's something awful, so hold onto your hats,' continues Izzie. 'Between sobs, he confessed to leaning over a bridge and throwing stones onto a railway track. A passing man went mad, shouting he'd cause a terrible accident. Jeremy ran home, terrified to tell his strict parents. I was the first person he ever told.'

'Flipping heck, is that it? How disappointing. I was expecting murder and mayhem. How old was he at the time?' Martha asks.

Izzie gives a wry laugh. 'The poor wee mite was only five, but nearly fifty when I saw him, after years of unnecessary guilt and anguish. I said what he did was nothing, blown out of all proportion in a child's mind.

'I told him not to waste another minute of his precious life, and asked if he'd consider throwing stones onto a railway track nowadays. He gave such a heart-warming laugh I still get a glow when I remember.

'He wrote a letter forgiving his five-year-old self, the passerby for being so harsh with a young boy, and his parents for being so strict he didn't dare tell them.'

Martha realises what Izzie has in mind. 'And he burnt the letter, didn't he?'

'Full marks to you. Have another sausage as a prize! Anyway, to get to the point, we all had similar problems before we asked for help: We were often manipulated and gave people silent permission to take advantage. It often stems from keeping a dominant person happy and pleasing them, even against our better judgement.

'As we are smaller in stature as children, a dominant personality is like a giant and the effect is stronger. Maybe as little girls, we kept everyone happy and carried on doing it without knowing. We say yes when we want to say no.'

'Tell me about it.' says Carlotta: 'Every flipping day!'

Izzie lips twitch. 'Everyone we deal with can become the school bully, or whoever, from when were small, forever exaggerated in our minds. It doesn't have to be when we are children; stuff can affect us when we are adults, except the effect is sometimes less as we have more logic. Small children take things literally and at face value.'

'Oh, I get it,' says Martha, 'that's probably why I could never stand up to James. But who, or what, was the cause?'

'Let's see if we can find out,' says Izzie, 'who's up for it?'

Everyone is.

'OK, LET'S START WITH Martha. Close your eyes and take a few moments to settle down. Imagine someone is asking you to do something you don't want. How do you feel?'

Martha is silent for a while, before saying, 'Pissed off, it's the story of my life. Can you be more specific?'

Izzie grins. 'Let's play pretend. The phone rings. You pick it up, and it's a friend you haven't seen for a few years, who's coming to Brighton for a holiday with her husband, three children and a whippet. She asks if you can put them up, after all, you have a big house. What's your initial reaction?'

Martha looks annoyed. 'Bugger off and what a bloody cheek.'

'Yes, go to a hotel, you stingy cow,' chips in Carlotta.

'Would you find it easy to say no, Martha?' asks Izzie.

'No. I'd say yes, then hate myself, dread the visit, and be fuming during their stay, but on the outside I'd be as nice as pie.'

Izzie continues. 'OK, go with the idea of believing you need to say *yes* when you want to say *no* and think where that takes you. What's your earliest memory of something similar? Take your time.'

After a while, Martha says, 'It was a terrible bully of a girl I used to play with when I was seven. I was terrified to defy her. If I didn't agree to do what she said she threatened to spread terrible lies about me to the kids at school and everyone would hate me.

'Once, she kicked me in the shins, drawing blood. She told me I'd better tell my mum I fell over, or she would kill me.'

Izzie cringes. 'What a delightful child. How long is it since you had the pleasure of her company?'

'Years, to my huge relief she moved to Australia with her parents a year after we met.'

'Has she been affecting you ever since?'

'Yes, I'm sure of it. I've been treating everyone like they were her. That's probably why I've let James get away with so much. Oh, God, I feel so much lighter.'

'Take your time and then open your eyes,' says Izzie.

Martha is stunned. 'Bloody hell, how can something so obvious have taken me so long to realise?'

'It was a horrid experience you put away deep in the recesses of the mind, beneath many layers, not knowing the long-term effect it had. Portia and Carlotta, are you OK with this? If so, let's see if we can unearth any of your inner demons, which usually turn out to be harmless pussycats.'

Portia is next. Her main life-changer didn't occur until she was an adult. Her childhood was magical and could have come from an Enid Blyton book.

Nobody is surprised to hear her problem is Todd. She admits he went to France after a row that got out of hand. He wanted to go to Bella's nightclub after dinner one evening, but Portia was tired and wanted to go to bed: 'Now I think disagreeing with anyone may cause them to have an accident.'

'Can you see how it wasn't your fault?' asks Izzie.

Portia bites her lip. 'No.'

Izzie continues. 'Hands up anyone who thinks Todd's accident was Portia's fault?'

Not a single hand goes up.

'Come on, Portia. You know there's no connection between the two,' urges Carlotta.

'I suppose so. I guess I do feel a little better. I've never admitted it out loud before. It was too awful; I felt so guilty - as if I'd pushed the motorbike into that fatal wall all by myself.'

'Portia, you only wanted to go to bed, and it all turned into a row. Todd was childish to flounce off to France; it's not your fault. If we all gave into every bit of emotional blackmail, we might as well lie on the floor and be doormats. I've been there,' says Izzie. 'I was one step away from having 'welcome' tattooed on my forehead.'

Carlotta is next. 'I don't need to close my eyes. It's my lovely Mum and Dad. They're proud of me, and I've never wanted to hurt them and always strived to be the perfect little girl they've told everyone about since I was young enough to understand what they were on about. How could I not live up to such high praise?'

Izzie looks thoughtful. 'What would your parents think?'

Carlotta puts a hand over her mouth. 'Oh, God; I've been silly. They only want me to be happy. I projected all this nonsense onto them. Also, I sometimes wish they'd called me something plainer, like Jane, less to live up to. However, bugger it; I will give my Italian passion free reign from now on, just like my crazy dad. Watch out, boys!'

'We've made loads of progress, well done,' says Izzie. 'Now it's time for the next stage. Martha, would you like to write a letter to that bossy girl, telling her she will not ruin your life anymore. Vent your spleen, curse, swear, do what you like, she won't read it; write as little or as much as you want. Towards the end of the letter, forgive her, tell her she now has no negative effect on you, and you have a fabulous life and dazzling future, in your very own words, of course.'

Martha frowns. 'I'm not ready to forgive; shall I leave that bit out?'

'If you want, although forgiving someone doesn't mean you condone what they did. It means accepting they are human. We all make mistakes. None of us is blameless. When we choose forgiveness over being right, we give ourselves the gift of peace, which is preferable to resentment eating away at us. The girl who bullied you was probably being bullied. If you can't say you forgive her, maybe state you *want* to forgive her. Let your subconscious do the rest.'

'Portia, you could write a letter forgiving yourself and saying whatever you feel is appropriate to Todd.

Portia nods and picks up a pen.

'Carlotta, what do you want to write?' asks Izzie.

'Masses, and I can't wait to get going, my fingers are itching to grab hold of the pen. How could I have created such silly problems out of almost nothing?'

Izzie laughs. 'It's a skill we all have. Meditation and counselling haven't stopped me being daft or worrying from time to time, but my life is much more enjoyable than before.'

After frantic scribbling, the friends write the letters then throw them on the fire.

Portia is tearful. 'Goodbye, my darling Todd. I forgive you and also forgive myself for the argument. All couples have rows. I wish, with all my heart, the accident had never happened, but it has, and I must get on with my life. I'll love you forever.'

Swallowing a lump in her throat, Carlotta says nothing and throws her letter onto the fire.

And, lastly, the third note goes into the flames: 'Feck off Martha the Martyr and welcome Martha the Marvellous!'

'Champagne and pudding?' says Izzie.

The girls go shopping

'OK,' SAYS IZZIE WHEN the group is together again, the next week. 'Let's take it one at a time and discuss progress. Martha, how's it going?'

'I love the horse riding. Yesterday as I was on a handsome stallion, Casanova, I noticed a tall man looking at me, well, staring. And the odd thing is he was wearing a Stetson, as in my dream. It was reminiscent of a scene from *Dallas*. He even resembled Bobby Ewing. As I passed, I glanced at him and our eyes locked for a millisecond, and I felt a glorious glow. It sounds cheesy but felt wonderful and natural.'

'Wow. Just like a Mills and Swoon novel,' says Carlotta. 'Was he on a horse, too, Martha?'

'No, just strolling, but he looked up at me as if sensing my presence, silly as that might sound. I love riding in the park. The problem is that I although I feel great on days out I dread going home, the contrast is awful.'

Carlotta grimaces. 'Oh, God, I'm the same. I can't go on much longer. I hate to be in the same room as Wolf. And meditation seems to enhance the problem. It makes me see I can't abide him. Hey, Izzie, I thought this meditation lark was supposed to make us feel better.'

'Do you feel more confident?' asks Izzie.

'Yes, you know I do.'

'Are you appreciating things more?'

'Well, yes, except Wolf, he drives me more nuts than ever. I want to throw a pan of mushy lentils over him.'

Izzie chortles. 'Meditation doesn't lobotomize us; it makes us more alert, more aware of our true selves. It won't make us like the poor housewives in the 60's who consumed prescription tranquillisers as if they were sweets, dulling their senses.'

'One of my aunties was on them, but I never knew until years later. I always wondered why she seemed so unanimated, go on, Izzie,' says Martha.

'Instead of popping pills, when we meditate, we dive to the purest most aware part of our being and heighten our senses. It can become more difficult to lie to ourselves, as we become more authentic, making it harder to be around fake people who read from a script that doesn't reach their hearts.'

'Like the worthies and holier than thou brigade,' says Carlotta.

'What do you mean?' asks Martha.

'Those people who go around acting pious, when you know they are a right bitch or bastard underneath.'

Portia chuckles; 'I've met a few of those!'

Martha looks concerned. 'Izzie does this seeing life more clearly business mean I could lose friends, not that I have many, apart from you lot. I never have much time. But I've noticed people getting on my nerves more, even James: I didn't think it was possible for him to annoy me any more than he has been doing. Will meditation make me anti-social?'

'It'll make you real,' says Izzie. 'If someone isn't right for you, it's harder to hide from the truth, and some people may fade from your life, and the right individuals and situations appear. It can also make us more tolerant, heightening compassion. I bet none of you feels as worried or insecure about moving on to pastures new, either alone or with a partner.

'As for making us antisocial, then no, but we feel less outside pressure about who we socialise with, how much and when. Think about how you felt before and how you feel now.'

They agree they feel much better, more alive somehow, in the past weeks.

Carlotta says, 'It's so true about choosing when to socialise. A friend called the other evening, at late notice, wanting me to go to the local pub. I was looking forward to an early night. In the past, I would have felt mean saying no, but I told her the truth, said I was exhausted and had a date with my duvet. She was OK with it, and we've set something up for next week, and I'm looking forward to it.'

'Great, Carlotta,' says Izzie. 'Some counsellors and therapists will bring you in for endless sessions to rake over the past, but if a meditation or relaxation technique isn't in the mix, it often creates a longer journey to a happier place.

'If we don't refresh our minds, getting out the cobwebs from all the nooks and crannies, we can keep going round in circles. Consoling people over and over does no real favours long-term, we can empathise, but at the same time encourage ourselves and others to move on from setbacks, disasters, disappointments or wrong turns. We need to get to the root of matters and meditation helps. Many worries and stresses leave on their own, and we don't need to revisit them. It's a case of good riddance.'

Carlotta laughs. 'Yes, bugger off and don't come back!

'Consolation helps some people, surely?' Martha asks.

'Yes, in the short term it can, but we have to be careful not to think of others or ourselves as victims. Nobody likes being an object of pity. Compassion is empathy without pity: Compassionate people don't see people as victims, but fellow souls going through painful and challenging moments.'

Portia says, 'I know what you mean. My best friend from school is amazing. When I bang on about Todd, she says she understands what I'm going through, but I'll get through it. She has faith in me, but another 'friend' who sometimes tags along says something like, *oh dear, poor you, it must be awful.* She makes me feel worse, like I'm stuck in the same sad place forever. But I feel better at the moment. I'll ignore that cow in future.'

Izzie says, 'I'm happy you all feel better, but maybe we should give it more time, see how you are in a few weeks, before taking any major life decisions. It's not always the best idea to take action from a position of stress or anger. Make decisions from a calm place within, wait until it feels right, from your gut and heart.

'We've already talked about how you want your lives to be. Let's allow things to evolve a little more, let nature take its course. You all wanted to get away from your partners when you came to see me. I know it's what Carlotta wants and Operation-Wolf is on the launch pad. What about Portia and Martha?'

'I'm about ready to move on from James,' says Martha, 'but I'm worried about money arguments.'

'My situation has become more complicated, but I don't want to talk about it,' says Portia. 'I want to have fun.'

Izzie claps. 'Great! Is anyone up for a shopping spree?'

Everyone is.

'Let's go. Where shall we head for?' asks Izzie.

'We can go to Sloane's,' says Portia. 'I can get you all a massive discount.'

'How come?' Carlotta wonders.

'Fabian's mum owns it.'

There is a collective gasp.

'You dark horse,' says Martha. 'Do they sell riding gear?'

THEY HAVE A FUN TIME shopping with the discount, stocking up on basics like tights, favourite makeup and skincare. Most of the clothes are too fuddy-duddy, even for Portia, who can feel the essence of her former zest returning. However, Martha spots dark brown jodhpurs in the equestrian section and tries them on.

'Wow! Those are amazing,' admires Izzie, as Martha models the form-fitting trousers which enhance her curves to perfection. 'You'll give some poor man a heart attack when he sees those. You must buy them.'

'I intend to,' says Martha, with a naughty wink.

After about two hours they pop into the store's cafe, Top Floor, for a breather.

'So what do you think? Be honest, would you have all come here if it wasn't for the 40% discount?' Portia asks, before taking a large bite of cream cake.

They all agree they wouldn't.

'Why? I know, but want you to tell me. I already know what you think, Izzie, you mentioned it the first time we met on the bus, and in our session a few days ago, after my revelations about Fabian.'

Martha looks curious. 'What revelations?'

'I promise to reveal all, but first tell me why you wouldn't come here,' says Portia.

Martha hesitates and looks uncomfortable before saying, 'I hate to sound ungrateful. However, it's all a little staid, so much so I can't believe it hasn't been James's first port of call when he's taken me shopping for my boring clothes. Whoops - sorry.'

'You've got it in one. It's bloody boring. It only does one style of clothes; sensible with zero sex-appeal, and they look like they arrived in a time machine, straight from the 1950's. I've seen nun's outfits with more allure. That's why hardly anyone makes a habit of shopping here anymore. Grace Brothers looks trendy in comparison,' says Portia.

Carlotta takes a sip of Earl Grey. 'Why is it fuddy-duddy now, when it was hip a while back? It must be losing money.'

'Until a few years ago it did well, now it's haemorrhaging dosh. Fabian told me about it recently. I've been mulling it over, and Izzie has been, too. His mum, who used to be obsessed with the place, refuses to do anything about it. She told me she trusts the manager, and it's the economic climate, but that's not the truth.'

'What's this manager like?' asks Martha. 'And what's going on?'

'Oh, no, he's heading towards us now. Act nonchalant,' whispers Portia as a tall, skinny character with oily slicked-back dark hair, and a narrow moustache slithers towards them with an obsequious grin.

'Well, hello, Mrs Belmont-Flowers. I trust you're enjoying your visit to the family emporium with your friends. How nice to have the leisure to take tea in the afternoon. We don't all have the luxury of such indulgences. I must get back to work.'

Carlotta observes him sliding away. 'What a creep! I don't trust him. He's got shifty eyes.'

'Neither do I,' agrees Portia. 'His name is Sidney Snape, and Fabian and I call him Mr Snake. He's probably the key to the store's problem and sorting out my life. My darling husband only married me because he was worried his allowance would get cut off: All that is overshadowed by what Fabian told me. Sloane's could soon be worth nothing, and I need to help.'

Martha wrinkles her brow. 'Your husband treated you poorly, marrying you under false pretences, so why do you want to help?'

Portia fills them in on the missing details then says. 'It was rotten of my husband's parents to threaten to cut him off. That stinks. Fabian feels horrible about deceiving me, and I believe him. We're going to work together to solve the problem. If he gets 49% of the store, he'll transfer 10% to me, to make amends. It would solve my money problems in one fell swoop and hand me a dream job. I'd like to know if any of you would turn down such an offer.'

Martha shakes her head. 'Are you kidding? Turn down 10% of London's largest privately owned store? Do I look insane?'

'I doubt anyone would turn it down. I've been mulling it over, and this might be a case for Barry Brillo,' says Izzie.

Portia looks curious. 'Who's he?'

Sorting out Colin Cooper

IZZIE IS IN HER OFFICE, sitting at a beautiful Victorian desk.

Doris comes in with a mug of tea and a plate of prawn and avocado sandwiches. 'Here's your lunch, my pet. You look like you're up to something.'

'Oh, Doris, this current group has just about reached the make-or-break stage: This time it looks as if all three want to leave their partners, which is unusual. You thought you wanted to get away from Benny at first, didn't you?'

'I did love, but when I changed, Benny fell in love with me all over again. He didn't like me being meek. Who knew? He appreciates me now, it's lovely. He still drives me mad sometimes, I'm not a bleeding saint. Anyway, you've got a mischievous planning look on your face. I'll leave you to it.'

Munching the scrumptious sandwiches, Izzie mulls over the obstacles of her three clients, remembering what one of the retreat gurus told her: *There are no problems, only solutions.*

The smallest obstacle will be getting Wolf to leave. Carlotta wants to be rid of her boyfriend but has said, more than once, she's frightened of him and is worried he might go berserk if asked to go. She's mentioned this a few times, so Izzie knows it's not an excuse. She needs to call in reinforcements. Grinning, she picks up the phone and dials.

After a few rings, the phone is picked up. 'Hi, this is Honey.'

'It's Izzie. I need your help and think you'll enjoy it. Can you come over this evening?'

'Darling, I'd love to. The sugar daddy is due to go on holiday with his family for a month. I can't wait for him to go; I've been with him too long, over ten years. I'm bored stiff. I'll have to cancel a date to make it, but I'll be over around seven. Have the ice-bucket ready and let's have an Indian takeaway.'

OVER A FEAST OF CHICKEN tikka masala, naan bread and sag aloo washed down with ice-cold rose wine, they discuss the Exit-Wolf plan.

Honey plans to seduce Wolf and lure him to her flat. If all goes well, he'll come and stay with her, having no qualms about letting Carlotta down. Before the sugar daddy comes home, Honey will ask Wolf to leave. Having seen a photo of him, Honey thinks she can cope. 'Wow! He looks a bit like Johnny Depp. And he's a few years younger than me; it'll be a change to have a toy boy.'

Izzie can't see the Depp resemblance and doesn't fancy Wolf one single bit, but she's not going to thwart a good plan. We can't all have the same taste. Many people thought her first husband was handsome. Izzie's mum could never see it. Recently Rose phoned to tell Izzie she'd seen Tim riding a bike and he looked like a wizened monkey.

'It must have been about to rain, Mum.'

Izzie pulls herself back to the present: If the Wolf Song plan doesn't work, they'll go back to the drawing board. Based on what Carlotta told her, Izzie reckons it'll be a cinch. And after about two weeks, Honey will ask him to leave.

'Is Carlotta in on this?' asks Honey.

'Yes, of course.'

'Then let's refine the plan, after pudding. I adore gulab jamun; I want mine with vanilla or chocolate ice-cream. You'd better have some in the freezer.'

WOLF IS ON THE SOFA watching *The Simpsons*. The marijuana makes it even funnier. He should stop the weed; he knows it makes him lazy. He's also bored. Carlotta makes life so easy that he can't be arsed to do much. And Cindy had been a pushover, too. He'd love to have an exciting girlfriend.

He hears a knock. Reluctantly pulling himself up, he shuffles towards the front door. Opening it, he sees a ravishing woman with a body like Jessica Rabbit. This babe is a goddess. And check out the size of those boobs, straining under the tight t-shirt.

Thinking *yes, yes, yes,* he says, 'Yes?'

'Oh, please have you got a map I can look at?' asks Honey, looking tearful. 'I'm lost on my way back to London.'

'Come on in.' Colin feels his luck changing and his trousers getting tight. What a hottie.

An hour later Honey is on the road to London, Wolf beside her. Two days later he comes back to Carlotta's to pick up his clothes and albums. He's moving out.

One down and two to go.

Barry Brillo

'SO, WHAT'S THE LATEST, Izzie?' asks Barry Brillo, slurping builder's tea from a chipped mug and adding lashings of brown sauce to a sausage sandwich.

Barry always refuses to meet Izzie in any of her 'swanky places' and insists on his favourite cafe, the Rumbling Tum, in Fulham.

Barry is a retired detective inspector, turned private investigator. He's helped a few of Izzie's clients, women and men, escape from difficult partners. He will only take a case if he believes the person he's investigating is 'doing the dirty' on someone and deserves the karma.

Izzie likes Barry, who reminds her of Columbo and seems to model himself on the scruffy, but canny character. Izzie finishes a mouthful of bacon butty, before telling him about Sloane's.

Barry looks pensive, takes a swig of tea, then says, 'Let's check I've got this right, Izzie. Fabian's mum almost owns the place outright. It hasn't done well for a few years, and the manager is blackmailing her. How long has he been there?'

'About four years, but I need to check.'

'No love, I'll check, that's what I'm paid for. And, what about my fee, the usual method?'

'Yes, Barry; when we sort this out, you'll have at least three people I'm guessing will be glad to pay you, Fabian, his mum, and Portia, so they can all chip in if they want.'

'Yes love, that's fine.'

Barry Brillo, apart from expenses, only accepts pay if he gets results. It reminds Izzie of traditional Chinese doctors who only charged patients when they were well. Barry doesn't lose out; most of the clients are thrilled with his services.

Izzie first met him when a stalker was hounding her. Barry soon discovered the man was in the UK illegally and was not only bothering Izzie but a few others. A quick word in the creep's ear made him terrified to glance at another woman other than his long-suffering wife. Barry avoided mentioning Izzie's name; she could sleep in peace. He also sent anonymous notes to the other victims saying a particular person would not be bothering them again.

'Have you any ideas?' Izzie asks.

'Yes, love, this manager sounds like he thinks he's God's gift to women. I'll do some research and get back to you soon.'

Barry hasn't got where he is by procrastinating. That afternoon he heads to Sloane's to investigate Sidney Snape, and locates him in the lingerie department, checking out the bra displays and looking interested in the Busty Babes range - DD and above. He is a sleazy looking character. Barry takes a few photos on his spy camera.

He trails Snape for a few days and discovers he visits the Queen of Tarts, for a wee dram or three before heading to the tube and his wife and two children in Purley.

Barry forces himself to enjoy a few pints during the evenings he observes his target.

IZZIE IS EMERGING FROM a relaxing geranium scented bubble bath when the phone rings.

'Hello, love. It's Barry. Here's the news so far.'

'Great, Barry. Fire away.'

'Snape is a distant cousin of the principal shareholder of a rival store, Fortwoods and Basin, who've been doing unusually well. A coincidence? Probably not. I've no lead on the black-mail situation yet. However, having observed Sidney, he's easily flattered, boastful and fond of a few snifters, mainly single malt whisky. And he plays golf.'

'What's the relevance of golf?'

'People close multi-million-pound deals playing the game. Golf courses can carry more clout than boardrooms and even bedrooms, and divulge as many or more secrets than the latter. I'm surprised you don't know that.'

'Yes, I suppose you're right, Barry. When I worked at the bank, the manager spent more time on a golf course, than he did in the office, but I always thought he was escaping from the horrid sub-manager. I had a few lessons when I was married to Crispin, but I was terrible. How will it benefit the Sidney situation?'

'I'm friends with Jane Racy, who owns Racy's nightclub.'

'Oh, I know her,' says Izzie. 'She's an attractive dark-haired Irish woman, in about her mid-thirties.'

'That's her. Well, I want her to ask Sidney to play a round with her.'

'Play around with Sidney? What a hideous idea. Jane Racy won't go for that. She's too classy.'

Barry laughs. 'No love, two words, not one; play *a round* of golf. I bet Jane could get Sidney to let a secret or two slip.'

When she puts the phone down Izzie sits on the sofa to digest the conversation. Barry is a miracle worker. Izzie can't wait for the next instalment. Her life is much more interesting than when she lived with Tim, bless him. He married the girl from Crypt's, and they had twins. Izzie doesn't understand how he coped when they were toddlers. She wonders if he had put *have two children* on one of his lists.

AS SOON AS BARRY IS confident of Snape's routine, he meets Jane: She owes him one, owning Racy's nightclub outright, thanks to his services. It formerly belonged to her ex-husband, Ron Racy. When they married the club was on its uppers, due to him gambling away the profits. Jane, probably the best networker in London, worked like a Trojan while her husband philandered his way around town, leaving most of the work to his wife. When Jane decided enough was enough and asked for a divorce, Ron tried to keep the club all to himself. Some detective work from Barry revealed some creative tax dodging on Ron's part.

Jane's soon to be ex-hubby was advised to transfer the club to Jane or languish in prison for a while. No contest.

'What can I do for you, Barry?' Jane asks over a grilled Dover sole lunch in Wheelings, accompanied by a bottle of Chablis. She'd refused to meet him in the Rumbling Tum.

'Well, Jane it's like this: I need you to flatter a sleaze-bag to get some info out of him, and maybe a bit of leverage would be nice. I know he loves to play golf and he also stops off in The Queen of Tarts most evenings after work for a few snifters.'

Jane takes a sip of Chablis. 'Yes, and?'

'I thought you could offer him a game of golf, massage his ego and take it from there.'

'As long as that's all you want me to massage then fine, I'll do it.'

'Yes, Jane, that's all. If we need to seduce him via the bedroom, it will be time to call in Pamela Bordello. Now, here's the story of sleazy Snape and this is what I want you to find out...'

JANE SHIMMIES INTO the Queen of Tarts, wearing a slinky emerald-green dress, high heels, bright red lipstick, and a sultry smile. She spots the target draped over the bar, like a lounge-lizard. She saunters up to the barman and, in a husky tone, asks for a Kir Royale.

Snape leers. 'I'll get that for the lovely lady, put it on my tab.'

'Oh, how sweet of you, finding a gentleman is lovely. I'm Jane. I love your suit. I've always adored hound's-tooth check on a man.'

After ten minutes of small talk and flatter, Jane gets onto the subject of golf. 'I'm disappointed. I was due to play at Bunkers of Berkshire tomorrow, but my partner has let me down.'

Sidney falls neatly into the trap. 'I love golf. I'll play with you.'

'Oh, I couldn't impose. I can't drag you from work, Sloane's depends on you.'

'I'm the manager; it's easy to take a little time for myself. Shall I pick you up or meet you at the course?'

Jane doesn't hesitate. 'Meet me at the course.'

James Hoare is worried

THE SUN SHINES. JAMES is driving home after adding a magnificent mock-Tudor house, with huge gardens, in Chichester to the agency's portfolio. The commission will be high, and he already has a buyer. So why isn't he happy? Something is niggling at him, more than his almost non-existent guilty conscience usually allows. Even an extra shot of gin in pre-dinner G&T's hasn't lessened nagging worries.

He's not sure he is still in the driving seat. For years he's been able to manipulate Martha as if she was a ventriloquist dummy, but lately, he's noticed defiance and spirit. Maybe even a touch of derring-do.

And what's with those jeans she wears now? She looks good in them, but he won't tell her that. Those dull outfits he chose for his wife over the years lowered her confidence; made her want to stay in the background of life, where he's always wanted her. He needs to be in control. There's no way he wants a repeat of his childhood, his mum ruled with a rod of iron.

He hated watching his father always cowed and diminished by a domineering wife, who makes Hyacinth Bucket (*it's Bouquet!*) seem a mere pussycat.

The phone rings. James jumps out of his skin. He only got his first mobile a few days ago, a Motoroamer 100BC.

'James's Estates, can I help?'

'James, me old mate, it's me, Tony. I've got awful news. That gold mine we invested in was a scam. The shares are worth nothing, nada. The missus will kill me. I talked her into spending our retirement fund on them. Meet me at the Hangman's Noose at 8 pm, and we can drown our sorrows in a few snifters, and hopefully come up with a salvage plan or an escape route.'

'There must be a mistake.' James's heart sinks to his feet.

'No mistake, mate. It was on the news, and they've already arrested some of the perpetrators. Plus, I phoned our stockbroker, he invested even more than us. He said he's driving to Beachy Head, and not for a picnic.'

'Shit. See you later.' James ends the call to his old school friend. He is suicidal himself. It's not far to Beachy Head; they could all jump together. The shares that would make him a multi-millionaire are bloody worthless. It must be a mistake, or Tony is winding him up; no not his style. They'd had a tip-off to invest in the Phools Goldmine, but it was all a big fat scam.

For months the shares climbed up and up, and he was on a high. They've been plunging, but he hoped it was temporary. He'd planned to cash them in after a few more months when they went stratospheric.

What can he do? With the help of Rick Cheatham, a lawyer and friend, he remortgaged the house to buy the shares, forging Martha's name on the documents. At least Tony had the sense, and the balls, to tell his wife.

James isn't sure but has an inkling Martha wants a divorce. She's refused any rumpy-pumpy recently. Massive panic overtakes him. He feels a pain in his chest. It fades: Must be indigestion. If she gets a glimpse of the deeds, he's dead.

Calm down; he's not without options. Over the years he's been siphoning off money from house sale commissions into a secret safe deposit box. He could pay back the mortgage and Martha would never know. His escape route would be gone, and he'd lose his rainy-day fund, but it's a better option than the dreadful alternative of being found out. And it's not only raining now; it's a bloody hurricane.

Tomorrow he'll sort it out.

After a restless night, he phones his lawyer to organise a meeting to get the remortgage papers reversed as if they'd never happened; he has no idea how Rick managed it and hadn't wanted to know. Ignorance is bliss.

'Hello, Can you put me through to Rick Cheatham please?'

'Oh, I'm sorry Sir, have you not heard the news? He was attacked by a shark, scuba-diving off the Great Barrier Reef. He's not expected to survive and is on life-support.'

James ends the phone call. What is happening? His life is falling apart. Is this the karma malarkey Martha keeps banging on about lately? Oh, shit. He'll either get his money and run away or be attentive to his wife to play for time.

For now, he decides on the latter.

The trials of Wolf Song

ALTHOUGH WOLF SONG enjoys living with Honey, he can't help being miffed Carlotta hasn't tried to get him back. When he motored to pick up his gear, she wasn't even there, and there was a note on the kitchen table telling him to drop his keys through the letterbox when he left.

Wolf headed straight for a mirror to check his looks hadn't faded. Phew, no - still handsome.

He borrowed Honey's Golf GTi for the move, and as it didn't have much room, packed half his belongings and left the rest behind with a note saying to dump the discarded pile. Somehow most of the clothes he'd worn with Carlotta were not suited to life with his new love. He wasn't going to risk being lazy with his appearance, and his hippy-dippy clothes wouldn't impress Honey.

He drove away without a backwards glance and had no idea Carlotta was next door with Nerys, peeking from behind the net curtains. As the car went out of view, they cracked open a bottle of cava, cranked up 'I Will Survive' on the ghetto blaster and danced around the room.

'Good bloody riddance,' said Carlotta, between jubilant giggles. 'He'll get a shock when Honey throws him out. It feels like a huge weight has come off my shoulders. I'm no saint, but he was taking the piss. I wonder how Honey will cope with him.'

TO HONEY'S SURPRISE, she enjoys being with Wolf, and he's back to being Colin Cooper.

'Why do you call yourself Wolf Song? It can't be your real name unless your parents were hippies.'

Wolf feels stupid. 'It suited my poetic leanings.'

'You've only had one poem published, and it's crap, but you're good in bed, so get back here now.'

'Yes, Honey.'

'If this relationship is going to continue, I'm not calling you Wolf Song. What's your real name?'

'Colin Cooper.'

'Much better, right, are you up for round two?'

Grinning like the Wolf he once was, Colin heads for the four-poster and Honey's luscious curves.

They are surprisingly compatible, and Honey refuses offers of dates, only continuing the dutiful daily chat with her holidaying sugar daddy: One evening, on the phone, he says, 'Tell me what you will do to me when I get back, Honey.'

She feels sick and can't face getting into bed with him ever again, even if she imagines diamonds, the idea of his flabby, wrinkled bottom, after Wolf's firm and pert derriere is a contrast too far. She wonders if she can live without the sugar daddy money.

The flat is hers: that was how he'd lured her. It's small, with two bedrooms, but in a prime location. She could sell it and move to a more substantial property further out of London.

No, scrap that idea, she loves her bijoux pad. But they need well-paying jobs. Hmm, London plumbers can make loads of money. Oh, my God, she's fallen for him, she has. She's not meant to know he's a plumber: An idea forms.

She heads for her jewel box and picks out the faux sapphire pendant everyone always believes is real. She goes to the bathroom and drops it down the plughole in the wash basin. Then she runs into the living room, where Colin reclines on the sofa, reading *Viz*.

'Colin, help. I've dropped my valuable pendant down the plughole. And it's Sunday; we'll never get a plumber. What can I do?'

Colin arises, Godlike, from the sofa. It's time to be a hero. And hang the consequences - what a woman. 'Hold on; I'll get my tools.'

'What tools do you need to be a poet, apart from pen and paper?'

Colin is so eager to please Honey he leapt to be a hero as soon as there was a problem. With Carlotta, he was in such a state of ennui and inertia that although he felt a bit guilty when she called in a plumber to mend the loo he was too keen on keeping his cover to own up to anything. If there had been a danger of flooding, he *might* have admitted it.

Like an assassin, hiding a gun, he keeps a few tools buried at the bottom of his suitcase and soon has the U-bend off and the pendant rescued.

'Oh, Colin, you clever thing,' gushes Honey. 'How did you know what to do?'

'I trained as a plumber.'

'Why did you give it up?'

'No reason, I just wanted to be a poet.'

'Don't believe you.'

Colin reddens. 'I didn't want to turn off the women. It's not a sexy job.'

'It is to me, so get your tool belt on, and mend that annoying dripping tap in the kitchen. It's been driving me nuts. And tonight I'm taking you out to dinner for the last time.'

Colin feels sick; he can't lose his Honey. 'Are you throwing me out?' he asks, eyes filling with tears, much to his embarrassment.

Honey feels an inward glow. There's her answer; he likes her as much as she does him. Those tears aren't false; she's an expert on the crocodile variety. 'No, I'm not throwing you out, but I'm never paying for you again, you will earn your keep. I've never supported a man, and I'm not starting now. We'll make plans tonight over dinner in Da Vinci's.'

Colin beams.

OVER A BOTTLE OF RED and plates of risotto, they enjoy a heart-to-heart, looking so cosy a waiter puts a fragrant red rose on their table, saying, 'For the lovers.'

Colin decides he needs to confess. 'Carlotta didn't throw me out. I left her.' He'd told Honey that Carlotta was chucking him out, so he didn't seem such a cad when he said *yes* as soon as Honey invited him to stay with her for a while.

'Why?'

'I fell in love with you, Honey.'

'When did that happen, you couldn't have loved me when you first got in the car.' She crosses her fingers. She knows he only accompanied her that first day out of sheer lust and the love came afterwards. It seems important he doesn't lie.

Colin holds her hand, across the table. 'I fell in love with you the first morning we woke up together: you looked flipping amazing without your makeup.'

'Is that the only reason?' Honey is flattered. She looks good without her makeup, who knew?

'No, I love the way you're so unselfconscious, I love your laugh and your direct way of speaking, I admire that you're so strong and bossy, it turns me on, my pushover girlfriends were a bore. I enjoy being with you and feel comfortable. I want to work hard to contribute as much as I can.' At this last statement, Colin startles himself. 'Heck, I want to work hard, what a bloody surprise. What can I do, Honey?'

'We will launch the best damn plumbing business in London. I'm sick of selling cosmetics, and the pay is crap. And I doubt I'll get any more money from my sugar daddy.'

'You're giving him up, for me?' Colin has never been this happy.

'Not just for you; I can't get into bed with the sugar daddy again. If it's OK with you, I'd like to keep him as a friend if he's not too mad at me. It's not as if I've been exclusive; he's got a wife and teenage kids.'

'No, I don't mind,' says Colin, meaning it. He feels secure with Honey and trusts her. It's funny they've both told endless fibs in relationships but now can't tell each other untruths, Colin knows it's because no woman has meant much to him; apart from his lovely mum.

'Why do you always call him your sugar daddy? What's his name?'

Honey mulls it over for a few moments, with the help of a few sips of wine. 'It's because I knew I didn't want to commit and it was only temporary. Whenever he talked about divorcing his wife, I changed the subject. He had no intention of ending his marriage but presumed I wanted to marry him: The silly sod.'

'I still don't know who he is.'

'My sugar daddy hates his name, Cyril, and get annoyed when I use it. In the main, I just call him darling. He's an influential man.' Honey leans over and whispers in Colin's ear.

'Bloody hell, you've been sleeping with Lord Eastling - he owns huge tracts of ancestral land, probably stolen from the Anglo-Saxons. How come your affair hasn't been in the newspapers?'

'Because of his elite connections mainly, he makes sure his mug shot is never in the papers. And we've always been careful where we dined out. The main place we frequented was in a side-street, and we ate in a private room, accessible through the back door. Cyril paid the owner well to keep things quiet. And we had a few other restaurants with similar arrangements. Izzie met him once, but just thought he was some old businessman, as did my mum.'

'Wow, you sly vixen,' says Colin.

Honey winks. 'So, I've got the connections, and you've got the tools; in more ways than one. Do you want us to set up in business together? Your first job could be at Number 10: The prime minister's wife has wanted a new bathroom installed for a while. I get all the gossip. She wants a Greek theme. I can wrap Lord Eastling around my little finger. Apart from anything else, I know too much - he's exposed some juicy snippets in the throes of ecstasy.'

'You're a devil; I love it.'

'So, shall we set up in business or not? We could call it Taps and Baths of Mayfair.'

'Hell, yes.' Colin wants to do a lap of honour around the restaurant.

Honey is over the moon but needs to get something off her ample chest. 'I've got a confession to make, but I'm worried you'll hate me, and storm off, like in those romantic comedies. You know, when couples are getting on well then one finds out the other has been lying and the outraged party ends the relationship; only to reconcile toward the end of the film: So flipping predictable. Sorry, that was wordy, but I'm nervous.'

'Oh, I hate those stupid plots; Carlotta made me watch loads of those movies. I always thought it daft when the characters overreacted. Try me,' he challenges.

Terrified, Honey tells him how the entire thing had been a setup, with Carlotta in on it.

Colin stares at her, and then after an eternity throws his head back and laughs. 'Wow, I have a new respect for Carlotta, never knew she had it in her. And I bloody well deserved it.'

Honey wants to dance with delight. 'There is one thing we must agree on,' she adds.

'Yes?'

'I respect you being a vegetarian. It's your choice and an admirable one, but I will not have you telling me what to eat.'

'Done, oh, dear, I feel another confession coming on.'

'What now?'

'Every so often I cheat and devour a bacon sandwich.'

MEANWHILE, NEAR BRIGHTON, James is sidling up to Martha on the sofa. They are alone. Simon is out for the night.

'The last few years we've been so busy we've hardly had any time to ourselves, how about a second honeymoon?'

Martha can't imagine anything worse. 'We never had a first, and what's with the sudden lovey-dovey business?'

'What do you mean my turtle dove?'

'It's too late, James. I want a divorce. And I've met some-one.'

Shit laments James as Martha sails from the room: Back to Plan A, of emptying the safe deposit box and running. Who the heck has she met? And, bloody hell, her arse looks good in those jeans.

Jane Racy

THE DAY OF THE GOLF match is bright and sunny. Jane is waiting on the clubhouse veranda, sipping a drink and waiting for Sidney. She has instructed the barman to serve tonic water, every time she asks for a G&T. She also hinted she wouldn't be worried if his hand slips when pouring Sidney's single malts, and whoops, puts more in the glass than intended.

She dressed carefully this morning, choosing slim fitting purple golf pants and pink shirt, unbuttoned to just within decency. A new purple titfer perched atop her head completes the lovely picture. She knows she looks good.

Here is Sidney now, swaggering up to her, wearing brown plus-fours, a loud yellow blazer, and matching cap. She pinches herself in an effort not to laugh. Does he think he's in a PG Wodehouse novel, the old bean?

'Oh, Sidney, you do look the part.' *Of a total plonker.* 'Would you like a drink?'

'Yes, a Sporran Single Malt, if they have it. What are you having, pretty lady?' Sidney crosses his legs to reveal bright yellow socks, decorated with embroidered golf balls.

A few minutes later they're sipping their drinks, and Sidney is boasting about his handicap of fourteen. Jane looks impressed but doesn't mention hers of eighteen. She's not worried: her handicap has been consistent for a few years, with regular games and competitions. Through Barry, she knows Sidney is boasting of past glories: He hasn't played regularly for ages, and the fourteen is bound to be as distant as the memory of his youth and will be even more elusive with a few drams inside him.

She's right: He misses the first shot. 'Oh, rotten luck Sidney.'

'It was a practice swing. I always do that for luck.'

'Yes, and I'm Mother Theresa,' mutters Jane, out of earshot.

'Fore!' shouts Sidney.

Jane stifles a giggle.

She plays poorly, intending to up her game after nine or ten holes. Sidney gets four of his balls into the lake so Jane copies the cad by wetting five of hers. After he sends a ball careening into the woods Jane finds him cheating; kicking it out of the trees. She doesn't let him know she's seen him: The bounder. Anyone who cheats at golf is usually a cheat in life.

'It's wonderful how you got that ball out of the woods, Sidney. You're a skilled man. I bet I can learn a lot from you, and not just about golf. Have you got any business tips for me? I always want to improve Racy's.'

Sidney puffs up. 'You need to be a bit ruthless.'

'Tell me more, you clever man.'

THAT SAME DAY, JAMES is heading to London to get the money from his safe deposit box. He has his passport with him and a small semi-packed suitcase, with plenty of room for the cash, planning to catch the next available flight out, to anywhere. The fugitive is panicking about airport officials searching his bag on the first leg. But he is desperate.

Arriving at the depository in Knightsbridge, he's horrified to see it surrounded by police cars and the entrance blocked off with incident tape.

In a sweat, he runs towards the door, in the manner of a human battering ram. 'Let me in - my money is in there.'

'Step away, sir, or we will arrest you,' cautions a burly officer, holding him back.

'What's happened?'

'There has been a robbery.'

James hyperventilates; a sharp pain stabs his chest.

He faints.

AS JAMES HITS THE PAVEMENT, Sidney is mid-brag. They are on the fourteenth green, and Jane wants to cheer; his boasting has disclosed some tasty morsels, and she smirks as his ball sails past the target, missing it by at least five yards. 'I know a secret,' he announces, to cover his embarrassment, 'It's big, but if I tell you, I'd have to kill you. It's about the owner of Sloane's.'

'I'm sure that's not the only thing that's big, Sidney,' says Jane, in *Carry On* style, as she chooses her putter. 'What's the secret?'

'I might tell you over dinner tonight if you're a good girl. I've booked us a five-star hotel.'

The arrogant little shit. Jane has had it with this farce. Enough is enough, and she doesn't want to see his niblick again. It's time for Miss Bordello.

'Oh, I can't Sidney, what a shame. I have to be back in London for a big party at my club tonight: Another time? But a friend of mine who shops in Sloane's fancies you. She was excited when I said I was playing golf with you today. I can set you up with her if you want. She's gorgeous, here's her photo.' Jane pulls a snapshot out of her trouser pocket.

Sidney looks at a photograph of an exotic looking woman, with waist-length dark hair, dusky slanted eyes, huge boobs and tiny waist. He is in lust: Again.

'Who is this? What's her name?'

'Pamela Bordello; she was a waitress in my club.' Jane omits to mention she is now a high-class prostitute, who often works in cahoots with Barry.

'Let's finish the game, Sidney.'

She trounces him and makes sure the club records the score.

Sidney is miffed. 'I thought it was just a friendly.'

A cup of vile coffee

JAMES IS AT A ROULETTE table in the Lucky Nugget Hotel, in Vegas, emulating James Bond. He is drinking a martini, shaken but not stirred, and has a sexy and svelte woman next to him. She is wearing a tight, low-cut red dress. The other players look at James in admiration, as yet another pile of chips are shunted his way by the voluptuous croupier.

Life is good. He's winning and winning big. He hears a series of beeps. It must be the alarm on his multi-function spy watch: As he reaches to turn it off the beeps become louder and more persistent. He hears a voice saying, 'He's coming around.' It sounds like Martha. What is his wife doing here in Vegas? She should be slaving away at the office. He forces his eyes open, and it takes a few bleary moments to show a hospital room.

A hatchet-faced Martha is standing near his bed, behind a nurse. Of course, neither James nor his wife knows of the irony of both having delicious dreams and daydreams interrupted by the rude reality of spousal presence within a short time.

'Oh. I'm so glad my darling husband is awake. I was worried I'd lost him.'

The nurse feels James's pulse. 'Get yourself a coffee and sit in the waiting area please Mrs Hoare while we check him over.

I'm calling for a doctor. I know you must be worried, but we'll let you know when you can come back.'

Martha heads for the drink dispenser, relieved James is conscious. She wants to give the bastard what for and find out what he's been doing.

SHE WAS IN THEIR ESTATE agency when a police officer turned up. James had left the house early, telling her he was viewing a property in London and was taking the train. The officer said, 'Please sit down, madam. I have news.'

'Oh, God no, please tell me my son and Arabesque are OK.'

'Who is Arabesque?'

'My horse.'

'No, it's not your son *or* the horse. It's your husband. He's in hospital. He's had a heart attack.'

For a moment Martha felt sorry for James until the officer told her the circumstances.

What on earth was he doing in Knightsbridge with a packed suitcase and passport? He was supposed to be viewing a property in Cheyne Walk.

She sits in the waiting area, nursing a cup of vile coffee, questions zooming through her brain. She can't cope with this on her own but gives herself a pep talk, shaking off the mental chains of the old Martha the Martyr. Yes, of course, she can cope with anything, picking up a magazine she flips through it, ignoring the dull and annoying daytime show on television.

After about an hour a doctor arrives: 'Your husband needs emergency bypass surgery, Mrs Hoare. It's best if you go home, as he won't be allowed visitors for a few days. Is there anyone you can ask to stay with you? You've had a shock. Or do you want to book into a local hotel?'

'No, I want to go home, and I've got good friends I can ask to stay with me.' Martha realises it's true. She has Doris, Izzie, Portia and Carlotta. Oh, and Don: But maybe it's a step too far to invite her new boyfriend to the marital abode, while her husband is on the operating table. Martha envisages the knife cutting his chest open and wonders if they'll be able to locate a heart; she has seen no evidence of it in years.

Don is the man from the park, the one who looks like Bobby Ewing, and Martha has been seeing him for two glorious weeks, mainly platonically, apart from a few hot and steamy goodnight kisses. They revel in wonderful romantic dinners where they never run out of things to say: Unlike with James who is about to undergo surgery. How does she feel about that?

She ponders. Nothing. Her darling husband has pushed her too far, and there is nothing left. From the television in the waiting area she hears music, introducing the news:

'There has been a robbery at the safe deposit centre, Hoardings, in Knightsbridge. Armed robbers made off with at least ten million pounds worth of cash and other valuables. The area has been cordoned off. Not all boxes were pillaged or stolen, but it will take some time to assess the details. The management asks that any concerned customers stay away from the depository until there is more news. Please do not do what this desperate man tried to do this morning.'

Martha looks up at the screen to see James flinging himself at the door.

What the Donald Duck has he been up to? She heads to a payphone to rally the troops. Izzie is away for a few days, visiting friends and family, so there's no point in calling her. Martha crosses her fingers as she dials the others: She should get one of those annoying mobiles but can't face the idea. It's good news. Carlotta is at Portia's who orders Antoine to drive them all to Brighton. And Doris is due to visit tomorrow morning.

Driving down the M23 Antoine says, 'It's rather bad form, Martha, guzzling champagne in the back of the car while your husband is having surgery.'

Portia sees red. 'Not as bad as you sleeping with my husband. And don't push your luck; you're lucky you still have a job. Mind your own goddamn business.'

Carlotta sniggers. 'Game set and match to Mrs Belmont-Flowers.'

THAT EVENING, MARTHA tucks into a Chinese takeaway. 'These ribs are delicious. I'm glad you recommended them, Carlotta, they're a change from my usual sweet and sour pork.'

Portia wipes her mouth with a napkin. 'James's ribs won't be feeling too delicious after the operation. Are you worried about him having surgery and have you any clue what he was doing? I can't believe what we saw on the news.'

On one level, Martha can't fathom it either, but she wouldn't put anything past him. What is sticking in her craw is that James must have had a lot of cash or other valuables in the vaults to be flinging himself at the door in that ridiculous fashion. How much did he have stashed away to be so desperate to get at it? 'I know it might make me sound like a heartless cow, but I was more worried when Arabesque was ill recently. I can't feel anything for James, except fury.'

Simon was home when they arrived, and appeared genuinely upset and worried about James, but maybe he was more concerned about one of his money supplies being cut off. He's a regular customer of the Bank of Mum and Dad. But he looked as bemused as Martha about the depository. Whatever, she didn't want him hanging around the house when she was talking stuff over with her friends so gave him funds to go out for the evening, with a caution: 'If you drink too much don't you dare come back here, you can stay with a friend.'

'I DIDN'T REALISE YOU had such a hunky son, Martha,' says Carlotta.

Martha gives her a warning look, 'Don't even think about it, for your sake, not his. The last thing you want in your life is another lazy layabout. I'm sick of him.'

Portia laughs. 'Tell us how you really feel.'

'I know, a far cry from a short while ago when I was more submissive. 'How is the Sidney Snape episode doing?'

Portia considers, before saying, 'Barry Brillo got great leads from Jane Racy. The snake got tipsy, played a terrible game of golf and boasted his yellow socks off. Barry's not revealing any info until he's sure. He's been doing more research, and Pamela Bordello is lined up for tomorrow night. Fingers crossed he is so flattered, tipsy, and high on lust he spills the beans'

'That won't be all he'll be spilling,' says Carlotta.

Portia feels ill. 'I need more wine to get over that revolting image. Hey, Carlotta, how's it going with Wolf Song?'

'It's incredible. Are you sitting comfortably?' She explains all about Colin and Honey falling in love.

'What is she going to do about the sugar daddy?' Portia asks Carlotta.

'He doesn't know yet; he's due back from his family holiday soon; so the shit will hit the fan.'

'I can't wait to find out,' says Martha. 'And things are getting interesting with my dear husband: I spent years wishing my life was less dull, and I've got my wish. But this situation with the deposit box is driving me nuts. What on earth has the greedy sod been doing?'

'Was he was trying to run off with all your money? Have you checked the bank accounts?' asks Portia.

'Oh, shit, that will be my first job tomorrow morning; followed by a chat with my lawyer. I'm filing for divorce, then I'm off to Texas.'

'Do tell.' Portia tops up the glasses and curls her long legs beneath her.

Martha & the American

ON ONE OF MARTHA'S rides in Hyde Park, a man on a piebald drew alongside her. 'Howdy ma'am, It's a splendid day for it.'

Oh, My God, it was him, the Bobby Ewing lookalike - *and* sound-alike! Martha felt her heart thumping, hands going clammy and mind blanking. All she could summon was a feeble *yes*, and even then it came out in a pathetic whisper. If he'd harboured any romantic ideas about her, they'd have trotted away.

She was wrong; he invited her to dinner. It was a first to be asked on a date when riding a horse, and it felt right, there is nowhere she would rather be most of the time.

Martha couldn't be bothered with feigning cool and said, 'That would be lovely, thanks.' She was supposed to be home that evening, to host a dinner party for six prospective clients. But there was no way she was missing dinner with the mystery man. She'd deal with James's wrath later; he'd have to cope with the ingredients previously bought and sitting in the fridge. The image brought a broad grin to her face.

'Something funny?' asked the American.

'Oh, no, just looking forward to tonight. Shall we meet at the restaurant?'

I'm from the south ma'am, and that isn't gentlemanly. I'll pick you up.'

Martha gave him Izzie's address before he cantered away.

Eat your heart out Pam Ewing thought Martha, finishing her ride early for a shopping spree. She had nothing date-suitable with her.

She raced to Harry Nicholas, intending to buy a fabulous outfit, before realising she didn't know if they were going out for an informal or posh dinner. She hedged her bets, avoiding jeans and opting for an elegantly casual outfit. She chose brown velvet slim-fit trousers and a beaded fine-knit cream jumper with three-quarter length sleeves. To add hints of sass, she went to the cosmetics department and bought a bright orange-red lipstick, volumising mascara, and a sexy fragrance; Femme de la Nuit. The assistant said it drove her boyfriend wild.

'Wrap it up,' said Martha.

THE EVENING WAS PERFECT. 'Bobby' had reserved a table at the Savoy Oyster in Piccadilly.

Over their first glass of wine, she said, 'I don't even know your name. I'm Martha.'

'It's Don. Don O'Hara.'

From then the conversation galloped along.

Martha couldn't get over the fact Don owned a horse ranch in Texas, Silver Spur, which was struggling. She told him about her daydreams and asked if he had an outside hot tub.

'I doubt I could even afford to heat the water: Silver Spur was doing OK until my wife divorced me. She engaged a shit hot lawyer, and I was wiped out. I'm over here because I can't afford my daughter's boarding school fees, so I'm taking her home. She's at some posh place in Guildford, St Trina's, and doesn't know I'm here yet. I'm also dreading telling the head-mistress, Millicent Simpkins.'

'What's your daughter doing at school in England?'

'Her mum's English and it's the same school she attended.'

'Why can't she help with fees, if that's not too nosy?'

'My dear wife ran off with her hunky yoga teacher. They're using the divorce settlement to set up a retreat in Thailand and need every cent or baht. She accepted a one-off divorce pay-ment, so at least I won't have a future drain on funds, once, and if, my finances recover.'

Martha asked how he could afford a trip to England on de-pleted funds.

'It's work. I'm here checking out racehorses for someone. I need the dollars, and it fitted in with taking Scarlet home.'

'Your daughter is called Scarlet O'Hara?'

'I know, not my choice. My ex-wife loves *Gone with the Wind*, the book *and* the movie. I sometimes think my surname was the only reason she married me. The biggest clue was when she called me Rhett in bed one night.'

Martha found this hysterical and was charmed.

SINCE THE FIRST DINNER, they've seen each other sever-al times. Martha loves having a fellow horse lover to chat with, especially one as sexy as Don. Although they've enjoyed a few hot kisses, they've not taken things any further.

She wants to get the James situation sorted, and Don needs time with Scarlet. They're giving each other a few months and then Martha is going over to Texas for a working holiday. She can't wait. But first, she must sort out James, not to mention,

Simon; he is a talented rider. Maybe he can come and live and work on the ranch. In an outbuilding though, like Ray Krebbs, before he came into money. She's sure it will do a lot more for his wellbeing than that fancy drying out place.

Her imagination is out of control, although it is more real to her than reality: She feels more at home with Don than she's felt with anyone.

Pamela Bordello

SIDNEY SNAPE FEELS like someone has poured magic dust over him. First, he got to play golf with the classy Jane Racy, and now he's sitting next to the sexiest vixen he's ever seen. They're at the bar in Racy's nightclub.

'I'm so glad we're out together, Sidney. I've fancied you for ages and kept popping into Sloane's to spy on you. I'm offended you never noticed me. I'm often in the shop buying bras; I love the Busty Babes range.'

'It's because I'm so wrapped up in my work, keeping the empire running.' Sidney is amazed he could have missed this luscious creature - and in his favourite department, which is the only area he always makes sure is well stocked.

Pamela hadn't set eyes on him before tonight, apart from in the photo Barry showed her.

'Shall we have champagne?' she asks. 'I want to celebrate meeting you. I'm so glad Jane brought us together.'

Sidney orders Krug, to show off. He'd have preferred his usual whisky but is not risking doing anything to jeopardise the best evening of his life.

He checked into a hotel earlier, putting his new silk pyjamas on the pillow, not that he plans on wearing them for long. An hour in the nightclub tops before he lures Miss Bordello to his lair. She looks like she's gagging for it and won't take much persuading.

Little does the arrogant twit know it took five hundred smackers to persuade her; an investment Barry Brillo intends to get back - with interest.

'You have such sexy come-to-bed eyes, Sidney. I can't wait. Shall we go to a hotel?'

I'm such a babe magnet gloats Sidney. 'As luck would have it I'm booked into the Porchester tonight, due to an early meeting. It seemed sensible to stay in town. I'm conscientious about my work and hate being late.'

'Oh, Sidney; how noble.'

Another conquest, the noble one rejoices, sitting in the back of a taxi, Pamela draped over him. The driver is envious: The lucky bastard. He gets to spend the night with that wet dream, and I get to drive a cab and go home to my missus, who sleeps in curlers and a winceyette nightgown. Life is unfair. He screeches the cab to an angry halt outside the hotel.

TEN MINUTES LATER, Sidney is lying on the bed, clad in black silk. Pamela emerges from the bathroom, wearing a skimpy nurse's outfit of red G-string, white cap, red stockings, suspenders and a low-cut micro-mini dress with a red cross on it. With a seductive smile at full wattage, she sashays towards a panting Sidney, on skyscraper heels which make her long legs look even more like the gateway to heaven.

'Do you want what you see, Sidney? I hope you don't mind, but I love dressing up.' Pamela sits on the bed. 'Now, come here and kiss me, you naughty patient. You haven't been taking your pills. I might have to spank you.'

Sidney can't speak; worried he might explode, before time. As he pulls her down beside him, she says, 'You're a bad boy, and haven't cleaned your teeth: Do it, and when you get back into the room, we can play.'

As soon as Pamela hears the tap running, she pulls a syringe, and a small tape-recorder from her handbag, puts them under a pillow and dims the lights. Then she lies on the bed, waiting for him, long shapely legs apart.

A minty-mouthed Sidney emerges from the bathroom and almost faints from lust when he sees Pamela patting the mattress, inviting him to enjoy her delights. He launches himself at the bed, faster than a greyhound chasing a rabbit.

Pamela endures vile slobbery kisses for a while, before saying, 'You were such a naughty boy, Sidney for not taking your pills so I will inject you instead; into your bottom.'

Despite all-consuming lust, Sidney is not keen on this idea, until she says, 'And when you've had your injection, you can fuck me. Don't worry; it's only vitamins. You'll need the strength.'

Sidney lies across the bed face down and hears Pamela saying, 'It's only a little prick,' as she injects him with Spititoutanthol, a truth serum.

After what he reveals, with a little more persuasion of the foreplay variety, Pamela reckons Sidney deserves his fun, but he's so tired from the drug and all the boasting he falls asleep after four lacklustre thrusts.

She was right; it *was* only a little prick.

Barry will be pleased.

Barry Brillo is pleased

BARRY BRILLO HEADS into Sloane's, wearing his usual scruffy raincoat, and a big grin. He's just come from a briefing with Miss Bordello, which she seemed to have taken literally: Her skirt was short, tantalising Barry, who saw her red briefs every time she crossed her legs. It was a bit much for him to cope with; he's used to his wife's big knickers. When she hangs them on the line, they look like peg bags.

Pamela refused to meet him in his favourite cafe, claiming the smell of grease would make her sick, due to a massive hangover. She hadn't been able to resist a few glasses of Krug. And after leaving a snoring Sidney she'd toddled to a different bedroom in the hotel to keep another of her clients happy, the randy actor, Lou Brant: During the frolics, she consumed three double whiskies.

Barry guessed she earned as much in one night as he did in a month. She offered him a freebie, but he won't take her up on it. He'd feel embarrassed revealing his ageing flabby body, next to her youthful firm perfection. And, he would never cheat on his missus, he's comfy with her, and it's lovely to return to someone kind and homely at the end of the day. It's a necessary contrast to the bed-hopping, scandal and double-dealing dominating his professional life.

Added to what Jane Racy told him he reckons they've got Sidney by the short and curlies. Heading towards Snape's office, Barry summarises the findings in his smart brain. The golf game with Jane loosened a tight top on a jar. There were a few hints and clues due to Sidney's love of bragging to an attractive woman when he thinks he's in with a chance. Miss Bordello, along with her undeniable charms and a small measure of truth serum had loosened his tongue, unscrewed the jar top, and the contents had gushed out.

Sidney was a cornered rat.

AT THE SNAPE PIT, BARRY knocks on the door, before hearing a weak voice: 'Come in, is that my coffee?'

Sidney looks awful. He's slumped behind the desk, looking pale and puffy-eyed.

'Hello, I'm Barry Brillo, pleased to meet you, Mr Snape.'

'Have you got an appointment?'

'No.'

'Then what are you doing here? Hang on, I know you. I've seen you in the Queen of Tarts a few times.'

'I've come to change your life, and not for the better. Have a good time last night, did you?'

Sidney's face goes from winter-white to chalk-white, and he starts to sweat. Hang on; maybe this Barry person is friendly, perhaps he has good news. Maybe he's a head-hunter for another store. He knows he's grasping at thin, fragile straws. Crap, he's in trouble.

'Phone your secretary and tell her you're in a meeting and don't wish to be disturbed. I want a long word with you.'

Sidney plays for time. 'Can I get my coffee delivered first?'

'By all means, and order one for me, with some biscuits. I like custard creams.' Barry removes a small tape recorder from his pocket and puts it on the desk.

Sidney brightens. 'Oh, you're a reporter. What do you want to know? Looking for a scoop are you?'

'Oh, no, Mr Snape: I'm much worse than a reporter. I'm your nightmares come true. The high life ends today.'

An hour later Sidney has written out his notice, left it on his office desk, and is leaving the store, accompanied by Barry. The truth will out.

A FEW YEARS BACK, SIDNEY was running a small supermarket and was short of money; with a wife and two kids to feed. Tracy, a spotty teenager, from the local council estate, worked as a shelf stacker and never objected when Sidney pinched her bum. Such high-class flirting lead to other things and she got more demanding, wanting meals out and money to spend on clothes. Sidney could just about manage by pilfering a few quid from the till - until Tracy got pregnant.

Charming Sidney denied the baby was his and tried to disown the mother-to-be. Tracy's concerned brother threatened to re-decorate his face with an iron bar if he didn't either support the child long term or at least make substantial maintenance payments. Or, the worst choice of all, he could marry her.

Sidney was desperate and visited a distant and wealthy cousin, Arnold Basin, the owner of a posh London store, hoping for a handout. Arnold said no. But, Sidney's visit was timely.

Arnold was worried. Fortwood & Basin was lagging way behind Sloane's profit-wise, which he thought was due to the latter's original and innovative female general manager, who he'd stupidly refused to employ, believing her too young and inexperienced. It reminded him of Dicke Rowe turning down The Beatles. Arnold offered the manager more money to jump ship from Sloane's, but she was loyal to Mrs Flowers, who'd believed in her from the outset.

At a prestigious society party, Arnold discovered a tasty morsel about Fabian's mum.

He wondered how to use it, not wishing to implicate himself, then he remembered the recent visit from desperate Sidney, and it clicked into place in his devious mind. He contacted a scruple-free private eye, with a talent for taking candid shots, and engaged him to trail Mrs Flowers.

A week later, the sleaze delivered an envelope full of photos and negatives, in return for cash.

'Are there more? If so, you'd better hand them over, unless you want me to measure your feet for concrete shoes. I have friends in low places,' said Arnold.

The private eye paled and handed over a second envelope.

'Now, get out,' said Arnold. After the door slammed, he spread the photos over his desk and rubbed his hands in glee. He dialled Sloane's. Snape's secretary answered. Arnold was eager to get his obnoxious plot underway.

SIDNEY VISITED MRS Flowers and told her to sack her manager and employ him instead, or he would reveal a lurid secret. Terrified, she complied. Once Fabian's mum dismissed the manager Arnold 'came to the rescue', and employed her at his store. As well as his salary from Sloane's, Sidney received backhanders from Arnold Basin to pass on information, and in turn, Arnold told Sidney how to run Sloane's, to its best disadvantage.

Sidney never told Arnold that he was also blackmailing Mrs Flowers.

The London Leech, July 1996

JAMES'S PROCEDURE WAS more severe than predicted. He was scheduled for a triple bypass and ended up with a quadruple. His recovery was slow, and Martha wasn't allowed to see him for the first week. For most of the second week, there were always nurses and doctors milling around, checking up on him. Finally, she has him to herself, and can drop the caring wife crap:

'Hello, my darling husband, alone at last. How are you feeling? Dreadful I hope.'

'That's no way to talk to someone who's ill.'

'I don't give a shit, James, and you'll wish you'd died on the operating table when I've finished with you. I appointed a divorce lawyer the day after your surgery. She's known as the London Leech and bleeds people dry. She's been looking into your affairs and advising me. I demand to know what the heck you were playing at, re-mortgaging our house and forging my signature.'

She doesn't mention Barry Brillo, who helped with the sleuthing.

James looks panicked and reaches for the call button. Martha is faster and pulls it away from him. 'The key and number of the safe deposit box were with the possessions the hospital gave me to take home for safekeeping. The depository is open again. Your box wasn't touched until I arrived. Now it's empty, and I have eighty grand sitting in the safe at home. And don't bother sending anyone to steal it. I changed the combination.'

'That's not what they meant by safekeeping,' grumbles James.

Martha glares at him, and he knows not to push his luck and opts to play for time. 'I can explain. Come back tomorrow, dearest; I'm tired.'

'Well, OK. Meanwhile, you can amuse yourself by imagining the lovely time you'll have in prison. Sweet dreams.'

Martha strides from the room, with a big grin on her face. Let him sweat for a while. She has no intention of reporting him but doesn't want to be a pushover either. She will cut a deal that will suit her. The London Leech is a figment of the imagination, designed to taunt and terrify James. She's not wasting money on a rip-off lawyer and is using a more sensibly priced local one. Right now, she's off home to ride Arabesque, and then take a relaxing long hot bubble bath, before the phone call from America.

DON AND HIS DAUGHTER are back at Silver Spur. He'd worried needlessly about taking Scarlet out of school. She'd hated the cold and crumbling pile, but was scared to tell her parents, knowing how much it cost. 'Oh, Dad, I'm thrilled to be out of that stuffy mausoleum. I love being home. Please don't send me away again.'

Don is overjoyed.

After a luxurious jasmine scented bath, Martha fills him in on the events of the day and outlines what she plans to tell James tomorrow.

'You're too kind. Are you sure you're happy to brush off your husband's dirty deeds, and not report him?'

Martha doesn't hesitate. 'Yes, I am. I've wasted too much of my life and have no intention of frittering any more of it away with a drawn-out court case. Plus, daft as it may sound, I can't do that to him. Happiness is the best revenge. But, don't worry, he is not getting away scot-free.'

JAMES SPENDS A TERRIBLE night worrying what Martha will do. He's ready to agree to virtually anything as long as he's not done for fraud. He's relieved to see his wife the next day. 'Martha; my dearest, how lovely to see you.'

'Cut the crap James and listen. Here's the deal. If you don't agree to it, I *will* report you. First, we are selling the house, the agency and the cars and splitting everything fifty-fifty. I'm also keeping most of the eighty grand apart from giving you ten grand to live on while everything sells. We are getting divorced, and you will not contest it. I will live in America for a few months to see if I like it. Simon is coming with me and can live in staff accommodation and work the ranch I'll be living on with my new man. You are *not* pampering Simon anymore. The only thing wrong with our son is that you've spoiled him and didn't encourage him to get a job. He drinks because he's bored.'

'Now, hold on Martha, that's a bit harsh. The boy has problems with alcohol. Hang on a minute, what's this about a new man? Dash it, Martha, that's a tad heartless, you gallivanting about, while I'm lying here close to death.'

'I've got years of 'gallivanting' to catch up with, and intend to enjoy myself from now on, so there! And if I'm wrong about our darling son, we'll discuss again, but I'm sure I'm right. He never drinks at home, even though there's always plenty of wine in the cellar. He drinks too much when he goes out, to keep up with his mates. He's in with the wrong crowd. Anyway, stop avoiding the issue. Have we got a deal?'

'And you won't report me if I agree to all this?' asks James, looking pathetically hopeful.

'No. Now, sign this. And use your call button for a nurse. We need a witness.'

James can't believe he has got off so lightly. His chest feels lighter than it has in ages.

Portia, August 1997

PORTIA PUTS THE PHONE down, leaning back in her office chair. That's fifty beautiful pairs of jeans ordered from Paris. A good cut takes an instant few pounds off butt and thighs. And nobody seems to mind paying ninety pounds for the designer denim. She launched her brand, 'Portia B' a few months back, and plans to add more lines. Being head buyer at Sloane's is fantastic.

She's had the job for six months; profits are on the rise, and the Managing Director is impressed. They're having lunch today to celebrate.

'Aren't you nervous, having lunch with someone so high in the business?' her new secretary asks.

'Hardly, he's my ex-husband. I used to be Portia Belmont-Flowers. Now I'm back to being plain old Portia Belmont.'

'Wish I was that plain. There must be hordes of men after you.'

Portia pulls a face: 'Oh, God, no. I'm enjoying being me, myself and I for a while. Besides, I'm far too busy with work.'

FOUR MONTHS EARLIER Portia received a phone call from Todd's mum; he had died of heart failure from the strain of all the drugs keeping him alive: Ironic. Portia was horrified and crawled home to bawl her eyes out for two days.

After that something strange happened: She felt part better, part guilty. Confused, she phoned Izzie to meet up for a good chat. Over a few glasses of wine and a Caesar salad in Jim's Cafe on Sloane Street, they got to the crux of the matter.

In a deep and secret part of her heart, Portia had expected Todd to make a miraculous recovery, like in Douglas Sirk's *Magnificent Obsession*, in which Rock Hudson's Bob Merrick saves Jane Wyman's Helen Phillips from blindness. Portia had been punishing herself, crazy with guilt and remorse, despite the letter she'd written at the fire ceremony, which had eased the pain somewhat.

No more, but she will always carry Todd in her heart. He'd be heartbroken to know she's been torturing herself for so long. Izzie told her that guilt is a form of self-punishment and enough was enough: It was time to live again, and she's doing precisely that, up to the hilt.

PORTIA IS ENJOYING her clothes and embracing her favourite rock-chick chic. She no longer wears her long blonde hair in a bun or chignon but lets it be wild and free, to match her mood. Fashion is fun again and so is travelling on buying trips. So far, she's been to Rome, Paris and New York. Her friends and her job are a joy. And no more money worries. Thanks to Barry Brillo she now owns 10% of Sloane's and has a salary, so she can easily afford the mortgage on her adorable little flat in Fulham. Fabian kept his promise.

Sleazy Snape has gone and the savvy store manager, stolen by Arnold, is back. Portia looks at her watch: Time to meet her ex. She hopes he comes on his own, not with Antoine.

Arriving at Salt and Pepper, she spots Fabian at a table for two, waving to get her attention. 'Hello, darling, I ordered Lanson.'

'Lovely, but only the one glass for me, thanks. I've got to get back to work. I want to sort out a delivery of leather dresses from Rome.'

'Loosen up; we're celebrating. Here's to Barry Brillo.'

Portia laughs, 'Oh, God yes. He sorted out Sidney Snape beautifully. What a story! The sleazebag is working as a traffic warden, and his wife left him. The snake is now married to Tracy, and she's pregnant again. But I can't believe Arnold Basin got away with his dastardly deeds.'

Fabian takes a sip of champagne. 'He didn't. Barry visited Arnold, who wrote out a healthy cheque to Mum to make up for lost business, *and* handed over the photos and negatives. Snape and his revolting relative are bloody lucky they're not in prison and Mum never pressed charges, she didn't want it out in the open.'

'I get it; your mum didn't want *her* mum to know about her affair with that prominent MP, Jenny Danvers. I can understand that, but it's rich she gave you a hard time about *your* sexual preferences. It's a classic example of the pot calling the kettle black.'

'I know, and Jenny certainly didn't want it out in the open, she was terrified of her husband and children finding out, never mind the general public. Apparently, she suggested hiring a hit man for Snape and Basin, which explains why mum was in such a state.

'Also, I now realise Mum and Dad were worried about how many people I was sleeping with, not so much what sex they were. Granny lives in the dark ages, though. She never recovered from knowing her daughter must have had sex to get pregnant. Mum was terrified when Snape kept threatening to go to the nursing home with the photographs. She reckons Granny would have dropped dead from shock on the spot, not to mention what Jenny Basin might have done. It doesn't bear thinking about.'

'Were there many photos, Fabian?'

'Yes, and I reckon very raunchy ones. Mum goes bright red whenever I mention them.'

'And what about your dad, isn't she worried about him finding out?'

'No. Mum told him. He keeps asking to see the photos, hoping they survived: The naughty boy.'

Portia sniggers. 'Snape was a greedy bastard; he wanted his bread buttered on both sides, with lashings of jam. Not only was he sabotaging Sloane's profits, but was vile enough to add blackmail into the nasty mix.'

'I know. Sidney's such a slimeball. As if it wasn't enough to coerce mum into giving him a job he wasn't qualified to do, he also took payments from her, along with an inflated salary. *And* he was getting paid money from his relative, who owns the rival shop, to sabotage the store.'

Portia looks confused. 'I still don't understand: If he's not going to court and he's got the money he conned from your mum, why is working as a traffic warden? I saw him issuing tickets the other day.'

'Because Barry knew someone who would have no conscience about cutting off his balls if he didn't pay back at least half the blackmail money and destroy any photos Arnold may have given him. If Snape ever contacts Mum again, he's had it, or his testicles.' Fabian grins.

'Wow! One more thing then we can drop the subject. How do we know Sidney or Arnold have none of the photos or negatives?'

'We don't know for sure, Portia. But between Barry Brillo, Jane Racy, Miss Bordello and all the evidence they're cornered rats. And Mum told Jenny Danvers that Snape and Basin destroyed all pictorial evidence, beyond all shadow of a doubt, and to enjoy her family in peace, staying well away from assassins.'

'Let's hope. By the way, how's Antoine, does he still wear his chauffeur hat to bed?'

Martha, August 1997

MARTHA AND DON ARE sitting on the deck outside the house at Silver Spur ranch, drinking ice-cold beers, and chatting.

'What a year, Martha. I can't believe you've moved here, and not only for a vacation.'

'Neither can I, although it helps to have an American passport, so there were no problems with work permits and all that malarkey, not like the character Gerard Depardieu played in *Green Card*.' Martha loves that movie and must have watched it at least four times.

'Well, you could always marry me, now your divorce is final.'

'Is that a proposal, Mr O'Hara?'

'Yes.'

'I'm flattered, but let's leave it for now. I'm enjoying living in sin.'

'Well, OK, as long as your sinning makes its way into our bedroom - and beyond.'

'Try and stop me.' Martha is looking forward to an evening and night with sexy Don: Oh, God, what a far-cry life is with him, compared to her dull and sterile life with James; like switching from black and white TV to colour. Her divorce came through a month ago, and she is now a wealthy woman;

unlike her ex-husband, who is struggling. Martha grins as she thinks of how he's had his comeuppance.

FIRST, JAMES WANTED Martha to delay the house sale. He had a buyer in the running who liked Murdstone Manor but would pay a hefty premium if James modernised the internals and added a conservatory before completion. Martha refused and said all bets were off unless she got the proceeds of her half, as agreed, and fast.

Rick Cheatham recovered from his shark attack, albeit with a pronounced limp, one less arm, and severe scars. He had been flown over from Australia and was recuperating at Overhill, a convalescent home in Worthing.

James, still weak from the operation, paid a visit, with a bag of grapes and a copy of Jaws. He told Rick the police were coming to arrest him regarding the fake mortgage documents. Rick burst some stitches in shock. James relented, saying he was only joking, the danger was averted but at a high cost to himself. Rick owed him one and James told him the house situation.

Cheatham was impressed with the sum the prospective buyer had pledged to pay and agreed to forward half the current market value into Martha's account the next week, based on James's estimation. Martha knew the valuation was too low, but the amount suited her; she wanted speedy closure and accepted with alacrity.

Rick also agreed on a deal to co-finance the improvements, and James got a loan to fulfil his side of the bargain. Upon completion, the two schemers would split the profits. Rick offered his only hand to shake on the deal.

A week after the funds were in Martha's bank account there was a huge news splash. An old woman, who had been living in Heaven's Gate nursing home, died in the process of blowing out ninety candles on her birthday cake.

Amongst her possessions was a note confessing to murdering her miserable husband, by bludgeoning him to death with a rolling pin. She'd got rid of the body by pushing it through a secret trap door on their bedroom floor, which concealed a small deep dungeon. She said he haunted her from then on, appearing in his dressing gown every night.

The ghoulish nocturnal visits were terrifying and began with the sound of his slippers shuffling along the corridor. Unable to cope, she sold up, hoping nobody discovered her hideous secret - at least while she was still alive.

JAMES WAS BREAKING the top of a boiled egg, while his favourite nurse, the buxom and bubbly Tanya Totty sat on the bed. He was recuperating in a nursing home. It was Tanya who had driven him to see Rick.

'When the sale of the house goes through, I'm going to trade in the Porsche for a Ferrari Testarossa, I bet a ride in that would get you hot, Tanya.'

'Ooh, yes, how exciting.'

'Pop the telly on.'

Tanya tottered to the TV and turned it on; the honeyed tones of a glamorous morning news presenter floated across the room.

Police are investigating a murder at Murdstone Manor, near Brighton.

James couldn't move or swallow, and an explosion of Sunny B splattered across the starched white duvet cover, making a huge orange stain.

'James, be careful, you've just had a quadruple bypass,' shrieked Tanya.

Worse was to come over the following days, as pictures of the crime scene made headlines in all the local media. The prospective buyer was horrified when he discovered the house's grizzly past and backed out of the agreement. Word travelled fast, and there were no takers for the haunted house.

However, Phil Graves, the local undertaker, was unperturbed by Murdstone's dark past, he'd seen and heard far worse. Rubbing his longer-fingered hands in gruesome glee, he snapped up the house for a song. James and Rick ended up with much less money apiece than Martha. James could just about pay off the improvement loan, with only a scant amount left over.

After this dreadful experience, on top of his operation, James felt weak and employed Tanya Totty, to look after him, in rented accommodation, until the business, cars and other bits and bobs sold and he decided what to do. He lamented the loss of the planned Ferrari and felt sick at the thought of trading down, rather than up, in the car market.

Tanya was not cheap, costing him a hundred quid a day, but it perked him up to look at her. And she was devious.

When James was feeling a little better, and the agency and cars sold, she persuaded him to go on a world cruise: 'It will relax you, my precious darling, and I'll come along to look after you. The cost will be worth it, to get your health back. As long as you pay for my trip and expenses, you won't even have to pay my wages. And there might be other benefits.'

THE CRUISE WAS A NIGHTMARE. The 'benefits' for James were sparse, consisting of two half-hearted blow-jobs, and the trip cost him a fortune. He had planned to book a reasonably priced stateroom with an ocean view, but during a night of passion, when Miss Totty worked magic with her tongue, in more ways than one, she persuaded him to book an expensive suite.

Once on the cruise, she sulked whenever she didn't get what she wanted which resulted in him forking out a fortune keeping her supplied with all the clothes, trinkets and handbags that caught her eye. James suspected she wouldn't be a nurse for long. He was right.

When the ship docked in Southampton Tanya ran off with a wealthy octogenarian earl, who was on the cruise to get over his wife's death. 'Ran' is a little ambitious; she pushed his wheelchair down the gangway and towards the waiting stretch-limo. The chauffeur who emerged from its luxurious depths looked like a movie star.

James was tired, broke, and yearned for a quiet life. He missed Martha; he'd been a fool, never content with what he had. He needed a job, and fast. James now lives in Bognor and manages a holiday park, the same one Doris used to go to with Benny. He lives in a caravan on the site and is saving to buy a car. But there is one happy outcome; without all the puddings Martha used to bake, his tummy is half the size.

'WHAT ARE YOU GRINNING at, Martha?' asks Don.

'Oh, I'm thinking about James.'

'Hmm, yes, it's funny how karma has bitten him on the nose, whereas my ex-wife seems to love her new life. The retreat is a success.'

Martha looks thoughtful. 'Maybe so, but your daughter isn't talking to her, that must piss her off.'

'I guess, but Scarlet will come round, she's a good-natured kid, and I doubt she'll be able to resist a free trip to Thailand. She loves you though and is fond of Simon; despite their bickering, they're like a proper brother and sister. It was an awesome idea of yours to bring your son to live at Silver Spur.'

'Yes, it was, I had a hunch he'd do well here. I'm glad I was right. He still gets tipsy from time to time, but nothing like before. At least if he's sick, it's over a wooden floor, not on a Chinese rug, and he has to clean it himself. There's no Doris here, although I want her to pay a visit. I miss her, and all the girls. We catch up on the phone from time to time.'

SIMON HAS BEEN A RANCH hand for a few months, living in staff accommodation. He loves the life and has a fabulous time with the other workers. He is also practising hard for a local rodeo in a few months. His sour expression has sweetened. Recently he visited his Granny, in LA, for real, accompanied by Martha and Don. It was a lovely trip.

Don interrupts Martha's reverie. 'Are you sure about investing your money in Silver Spur? I'll understand if you want to back out. Don't feel obligated.'

'I've never been more certain about anything, well, apart from knowing I love being with you. I'm excited about our plans.'

As soon as Martha first arrived, she loved everything about the ranch, from the spacious but unpretentious five-bedroom timber house to the vast acres. Don laughed when she commented on the size of the land: 'For Texas the acreage is small.'

Arabesque seems to love it, too - she was flown over, at a high cost, but worth every penny. Martha rides her every day, grooming her personally, and they adore each other. They are here to stay, and Martha is confident to put the divorce money into saving the ranch. It feels right.

'The money situation is more like a dry riverbed than a flow,' warned Don. 'Maybe I should sell Silver Spur?'

'You'll do no such thing, Mr O'Hara. What if I invest in it, as a partner?'

'That would be amazing. I'd love it. Are you sure?'

'Absolutely, let's make plans.'

Over many beers and barbecues Don and Martha talked about the future and the cash-flow problem and came up with the idea that excited them both:

They would carry on running Silver Spur as a working ranch, adding additional buildings to house holidaymakers who wanted to be ranch hands for a week or two, like in *City Slickers*. She'd seen how the life was rejuvenating her son.

Simon and Scarlett were also keen on the idea, so everyone was happy and fulfilled, and life was fun again.

Martha raises her beer bottle: 'To Silver Spur!'

Carlotta, August 1997

'MY USUAL COFFEE PLEASE, Carlotta. Can I feel something brewing between us?'

'Only coffee, Daffyd. Men aren't on my menu for the moment.'

'But I do like you a whole latte. And can I have something sweet to go with it?'

'I haven't heard that one before. Just you behave and go and sit down. I need to serve another customer.' Carlotta passes the order to Nerys and smiles at the old lady who is next in line. 'Hello, Mrs Thomas. Scone and a pot of tea, is it?'

'Yes, cariad, there goes another broken heart. The men are falling like skittles; I can see why - you look lovely since you got rid of that deadbeat boyfriend.'

'Thanks, Mrs T. Now, what jam do you want today, strawberry, raspberry or blackcurrant?'

'Strawberry please, Carlotta. I've looked forward to this all morning. I'll enjoy it with my *Women's Friend* magazine. You bake the best scones in Wales.'

Carlotta has been working in the Crempog for nearly a year. Soon after Wolf left, she invited Nerys round for dinner, and blurted out, 'I love the cafe. How about employing me?'

Nerys downed three mouthfuls of chilli and two glugs of wine, without a word.

Carlotta felt foolish. 'Oh, you hate the idea. Forget I said anything.'

Nerys put down her knife and fork. 'You spooked me: I was going to ask if you fancied a job. I'm bored with the cafe; it's lost its sparkle. The Crempog needs a lift, and so do I. Are you any good at painting?'

'I was crap at art and dreaded it more than maths at school. I never progressed beyond stick figures. Do you want the ceiling painted like the Sistine Chapel or something?'

'Not that sort of painting, you moron, I mean decorating.'

'I redid my entire house over the last few years; a room at a time whenever Wolf decamped. I tried decorating alongside him, but the atmosphere was terrible. You'd imagine I'd asked him to go down the pit, rather than wield a paintbrush. My hardworking miner granddad wouldn't have put up with him for a second. Anyway, why are you asking?'

'I fancy giving the cafe a new look, inside and out. I got a quote from a local firm and nearly fell over. How about I close up for a few weeks, to tart the place up, then we can re-open - together.'

'I'm in!'

THE FIRST THING THEY did was give the outside a facelift. There was a spell of good weather, and the girls painted the front door and window frames a gorgeous warm coral. Carlotta found bargain folding tables and chairs to put outside.

'You're optimistic, or maybe delusional,' said Nerys. 'We've probably had our ration of sunshine for this year.'

They painted the inside walls the same colour as the door and windows, and treated the tables to new tablecloths, with colourful cake graphics; wipe clean to save on laundry.

They scoured charity shops and jumble sales for framed prints of people eating and having a good time. Their favourite was Renoir's Boating Party, and it took centre stage above the old stone fireplace.

Carlotta insisted on a decent sound system. 'We can't boogie to Tom Jones on that tinny old thing. I'll choose something good, so we can belt out 'Delilah' as we clean up at the end of the day.'

In the evenings, after painting and refurbishing all day, they made plans over numerous glasses of wine. They decided to dispense with a chef altogether and focus on scones, bara brith, cakes, croissants, soup, and sandwiches; all stuff they could prepare in advance.

So far, it's working well. As well as homemade fare, Nerys and Carlotta buy in delicious pastries from Jones the Baker, famous for his almond and chocolate croissants.

'I'll need to invest in elastic waist trousers, surrounded by all these goodies,' said Carlotta.

The usual accompaniment for the bara brith and scones is lashings of creamy Welsh butter and homemade jams. *I Wish this were Butter* is on request, and neither of them can imagine why anyone would choose it.

It is hard work, but Carlotta enjoys it. However, she decided against asking Nerys if she can be a business partner, not wanting to feel tied down to anyone or anything. The feeling of freedom is bliss. For most of the first month after Colin left, she stayed home, revelling in the Wolf-free vibe. And she threw all remaining packets of lentils in the bin.

THEY CAN ALMOST MANAGE the cafe between them, using part-timers for their days off and extra-busy times. Sometimes Carlotta's mum helps on Saturdays and loves every minute. Her dad comes in, but only to eat cake, drink tea and drive his wife and daughter bonkers with his teasing.

The Crempog is rarely quiet. From opening in the morning to closing at five o'clock, they have a steady stream of customers, particularly in their 'special' hours:

On Wednesdays, they have a Pensioners Picnic in the afternoon, a free bakery item with every drink.

'I couldn't believe it when Mrs Williams had three mugs of tea and three cakes this week,' said Carlotta. 'Yet she always complains about her weight.'

On Thursdays they run an After School Special for kids and their parents; everything a third off. It's great fun, albeit deafening.

'Those two women who kept telling their little boys to keep quiet were noisier than all the children put together, don't you think, Nerys?'

'I'm buying earplugs for next week.'

'And I'm emigrating.'

After a day on their feet, the friends often unwind at closing time and enjoy a good natter, over tea and cake. Their favourite subject is the cafe and its patrons; most are lovely chatty locals with lots of light-hearted local gossip.

The only customers they dread are the four friends who visit for tea and scones once a week; the girls call them the Misery Quartet. Their favourite topic of conversation is illness; the list of patients includes themselves, friends and relatives. Or maybe someone they met on the bus. They usually speak loudly, but when discussing private and personal matters they use a stage whisper - which can be heard throughout the cafe.

It reminds Nerys and Izzie of Les Dawson, in pinafore and curlers, chatting to 'her' neighbour over the garden fence. 'I've got that trouble again, you know, down there.'

The Misery Quartet stayed longer than usual this week; there had been a glut of surgical misfortunes.

'So, when my boil was lanced...'

'And her stitches didn't heal properly...'

'The anaesthetic didn't agree with her...'

'It's scabbed over now, but you should...'

Nerys says, 'I nearly fainted today, the way they went on with the gory details. I wish I could send them to the hospital canteen for afternoon tea. Or maybe they'd prefer a ringside seat in the operating room, slurping tea and scoffing cake, as the surgeon wields a scalpel. Anyway, any plans for tomorrow's baking, Carlotta?'

'I'll make the white chocolate and raspberry scones again; they were a hit. And your broccoli and stilton soup went down a treat today. There's none left.'

'Was it a mistake to dispense with a chef?'

'Did you enjoy the cafe the way it was? You were nearly always stressed.'

'No. I much prefer it this way.'

'If there's one thing, I've learnt since Izzie is that life flows more smoothly when we're doing what we enjoy. There is a happy atmosphere in here, apart from apart from when the Misery Four visit, and the customers sense it. They don't just come in for the food.'

'True. There is no point in working for myself and not enjoying it. Hey, how is your novel going, Carlotta?'

'Slowly, I've only written a few paragraphs. There's something I want to run by you, though.'

'Shoot.'

'The local paper contacted me the other day and asked if I'd consider taking up a column again, a light-hearted piece about the idiosyncrasies and minutiae of small-town life.'

'Go for it. And you'll get lots of inspiration from this place.'

'I know, maybe I will call it *Crempog Corner*, a bit like *The Archers*, but in print.'

'Is the pay good?'

'Not as much as I got from the national rag: but I'll put the money aside to visit Martha in America.'

'How is she?'

Carlotta slathers butter on a chocolate chip scone. 'She's a damn sight happier nowadays.'

'Not surprising. Now, down to some serious stuff - there is a dripping tap in the kitchen, do you think we should give good old Wolf Song a call?'

Carlotta laughs. 'We couldn't afford him now he's a posh plumber.'

Honey Potts, August 1997

HONEY PUTS THE PHONE down with a satisfied grin. Taking a sip of Chablis, she says to Colin, 'That was Mountain House School; there's a slight problem with a toilet that won't flush; one of the little monsters has got a toy car lodged in it. The headmistress asked for you; she's in lust, not that I mind: The more women who fancy you, the more trade. I made an appointment for tomorrow morning at ten, which will give us time for a leisurely start. I told them you'd be tied up until then.'

'Then we mustn't make a liar of you. I love it when you tie me to the bedposts. But why are you looking so smug? You haven't got to stick your head down a toilet.'

'You know damn well why, Colin my dear. We're coining it in, on our own terms. It's not as if you're only fixing loos; you installed six sinks and ten toilets in that posh school. I could skip when I think of the bill, paid within a week. We both have our self-esteem back. I'm not pretending to enjoy sex with some old fart, and you're not being kept by anyone, either. Life is better since we've been together.'

Colin and Honey launched their business, Taps and Baths of Mayfair, eight months ago, and it was a success from the outset, thanks to Honey's ex, who she still sees for dinner once a week; he may look, but not touch. Colin has no objections; Lord Eastling is their sponsor and invested a substantial sum in the business. He also rents them an office in the same building as their flat, at a low rate.

HONEY WAS TERRIFIED when she told the sugar daddy it was over, worried he'd go crazy. She waited until they were having dinner at his favourite restaurant, Lolita's, and he'd imbibed two glasses of wine. 'Please don't be mad: I've met someone, but I hope you and I can stay friends.'

To her horror, his eyes filled with tears, and he took a few sips of Barolo to steady himself. 'I was expecting this; you've sounded different when we've spoken on the phone these last weeks. I had a wonderful time while it lasted, my Honey. You're a beautiful butterfly I knew I couldn't keep in my net for much longer. I'm not a fool and know you wouldn't have looked at me if I hadn't been rich. I hope we can stay friends. Will you and your new young man be OK with that?'

Honey's was thrilled. 'Oh, I'm so happy you said that. But how do you know there is a young man involved?'

'Now it's my turn to say don't get mad. I used a private detective to watch you. He was a scruffy chap, but efficient, with an odd name; Barry Brillo. He reminded me of Columbo. Hey, why are you laughing?'

Honey told the story of Sidney Snape, and Pamela Bordello, and Lord Eastling joined in with the laughter.

Recovering, he said, 'I like the sound of Miss Bordello. Maybe she can be my next conquest?'

'You dirty old dog. Your friend Barry can fix you up with her. Now, how about giving me some business advice…'

BY THE END OF THE EVENING, Lord Eastling was an investor in Pamela and Colin's new venture. He wasn't daft; with his connections and Honey's stunning looks and natural public relations ability it couldn't fail, not even if this new boyfriend was only an average plumber, after all, soon they might need a team.

Apart from anything, he likes Honey, she's fun, and he wanted an excuse to keep seeing her. And he'd be able to tell his wife the truth; he really would be having business meetings, discussing Taps and Baths.

It'd be a relief not having the pressure to perform regularly; he was worried about the effect a new drug he'd been buying, at great expense, might have on his heart. He couldn't remember its name, Vigour, or something. Mind you; it was going to be big, and he'd bought shares before the price inflated too much and the market exploded.

It would be a pleasant change to sit at home in his dressing-gown in the evenings, watching TV with his wife, snuggled together on one of their luxurious sofas.

HONEY AND COLIN ACQUIRED their first green van, with Taps and Baths of Mayfair and a phone number, written in fancy gold lettering on each side. The jobs poured in, wherever water was pouring out in posh addresses.

Soon after, they began installing bathrooms; Victorian style claw-foot baths, and toilets with chain-pull cisterns were the most popular, then they got the contract for the school, and so the jobs escalated. Number 10 got its Greek-themed bathroom.

Now they have three vans and two other plumbers. Soon they might need more; Honey finds a new client every few days and goes through hundreds of business cards a week. She has no compunction about handing them out wherever she goes. When she comes home, she does the books, grinning to herself like Scrooge as she tots up the takings:

Honey is the most glamorous plumber's wife in the world. Yes, she married Colin a few months ago. Miss Potts is now Honey Potts-Cooper. Lord Eastling gave a moving speech at the reception; her dad was too shy but was bursting with pride throughout the proceedings. Her mum even removed her apron for the wedding - and ate more than anyone else at the reception: Held at Swanks.

Lord Eastling's wedding present to them was a week in Paris, staying in a suite at the decadent Hotel Extravagant.

Full Circle, December 1999

MARTHA LANGUISHES IN a deliciously warm hot tub, with her fiancé as they drink bottles of ice-cold beer. Don is wearing only a Stetson and a sexy grin. They're relaxing after an enjoyable day, training mustangs on their Texas Ranch. 'I can't believe my fantasy came true, Don. Pinch me; I want to make sure this is real.'

'Are you looking forward to your friends coming over for the wedding?'

'I can't wait; I haven't seen them since I moved here. Even my darling Doris is coming, leaving Benny at home. She fancies a girl's trip and doesn't want him cramping her style. I love her.'

Six months ago, Don asked Martha to marry him, for the umpteenth time, and she finally said yes. The ceremony and the barbecue reception will both take place on the ranch, around the swimming pool.

When she arrived, Silver Spur, like many Texan properties, already had a pool, but it was grim, Martha always expected a frog and a few fish to join in with her swim.

Five months ago, they splashed out on a beautiful new pool, next to the large patio. The crest of the wave was the wooden hot tub, which gets plenty of use from Martha, Don and the occasional visitor.

They installed a second, less lavish pool, near the staff and guest quarters. The old Martha would have felt guilty keeping the best pool and accompanying hot tub private, but the new one has no qualms. It's easy to say no once you start. She also says *yes* a lot, but only when she wants to, when intuition tells her. She now knows an immediate knot in the stomach is her cue to say the magic word *no*. The amazing thing is that people seem to respect her for it.

She remembers Izzie saying that when we are ourselves, we permit others to be themselves and people like being around someone who is being natural. Naturalness has more power than fakery, which never wins, long-term.

'You're miles away, Martha. Are you fantasising about our wedding night?'

'Of course, but I'm also focusing on my good fortune, which I'll never take for granted as long as I live. Shall we go over the plans for the nuptials again?'

Don groans.

IT'S TUESDAY 28TH DECEMBER 1999. The wedding is taking place on Saturday 1st January 2000. A country band, The Rambling Raspberries, will play for the first part of the reception, after which there'll be a marquee covered disco, with a lit-up dance floor in the second half, until midnight and beyond. The girls have requested their favourite tracks. Carlotta wants 'I Will Survive' as it will always remind her of Exit-Wolf. Doris wants 'Why Do Fools Fall in Love?' - Cheeky cow! Portia wants 'Karma Chameleon'. Izzie requested Van Morrison's

'Brown Eyed Girl', knowing how Martha loves the dancing in hats scene from *Sleeping with the Enemy*.

Tomorrow morning, as a surprise, Martha is taking a stretch limo, with cow horns at the front to pick the girls up from the airport. They'll spend the rest of the day and evening relaxing and recovering from the flight. Thursday night is the hen party, and then Friday is preparation day, followed by Millennium celebrations, then the wedding is on Saturday.

'I must be insane, Don, arranging so much before the big day. I'll look ninety when I stagger up the aisle.'

'No, you won't, you'll be high on happiness with your mates over here. You can rest on the honeymoon, well, not too much. But you can certainly spend plenty of time in bed.' Don gives a cheeky wink.

After the wedding, they're all spending a few days relaxing at Silver Spur before the girls return home and the newly-weds go on a honeymoon, to the Caribbean. They've worked so hard at the ranch this will be their first proper holiday together. Martha doesn't regret a moment of the work, her hunch had been right; the business is making a profit again, after all the dollars spent on it.

'OOH I FEEL NAUGHTY, travelling business class,' says Doris, but it's a decadent treat.

'I know,' says Carlotta, 'but it's appropriate for such a special occasion. I can't believe I'm away for a while. I'll probably get up in the night and bake scones.'

'Wake me up, if you do,' says Doris.

Portia joins in. 'Count me in. By the way, I feel a bit guilty leaving the store, scratch that; I don't at all. It's your fault, Izzie. Where's all that healthy guilt we used to experience?'

Izzie laughs. 'Well, if we were all thieves or murderers, guilt might be warranted, but feeling guilty about treating ourselves well is plain daft.'

'Don't you ever feel guilty, Izzie?' asks Carlotta.

'I do, on occasional sleepless nights when I wake at three in the morning, but these days I've mainly got it under control. What's the point of feeling guilty about something you wish you had or hadn't done or said years ago unless you own a time machine? If there's anything you can do in the present to remedy the situation go ahead, if not forget it, move on and enjoy your life.'

'I sometimes worry, on my dark days, that I shouldn't be this happy when there is so much sadness in the world,' says Doris.

'You're right,' says Carlotta, laughing. 'Let's all go back to being miserable. That was fun and did people a lot of good. We cheer people up when we're happy and depress them when we're not. There would be fewer wars if people focused on the good things in their lives. Happiness is a gift. Whoops, that sounded preachy. We're off to a wedding. It's time to party. Let's talk about fun stuff. What are you all wearing for the big day?'

Portia is wearing a raunchy royal blue dress, held together at the sides with large silver safety pins. 'I was worried it's a bit OTT but checked with Martha who said to go for it.'

Doris plans to wear a pink chiffon dress. 'Benny said I look lovely in it.'

Izzie will be in a long fitted crushed velvet cream dress, with mermaid hem, worn with a black boa feather scarf.

Carlotta has a sexy red mini-dress stashed in her suitcase. Since that time at Martha's, when James was in hospital, she's never forgotten hunky Simon and is sure a meaningful look passed between them.

It's a lovely flight and the time goes quickly in the comfy seats. They alternate between chit-chat, cat-naps, eating tasty food, and watching movies. They titter over *Deuce Bigelow: Male Gigolo* and are engrossed and moved to tears by *The Green Mile*.

They are too excited to settle down with a book.

Hours later, tired but happy, they walk into the arrival hall at Houston Airport. Portia spots Martha first, looking happy and beautiful in jeans, shirt and cowboy boots, her lovely open face a mass of freckles. She jumps up and down like a ten-year-old when she spots them.

When they see the limo, it's their turn to jump up and down and shriek.

On the road, the engine's expensive purr is hidden by excited chatter. 'Ooh, look at all that lovely blue sky,' says Doris.

They break the three-hour journey to Littlefoot with a visit to Benny's Diner. As they walk in they are serenaded by Bruce Springsteen, singing 'Glory Days.' 'This is sure a glorious day,' says Martha.

The girls tuck into fluffy pancakes and maple syrup, washed down with endless coffee. Martha takes a big slurp of the dark liquid. 'This good strong joe is just what I needed.'

'Don't be greedy,' says Doris. Why do you want a Joe when you've got a Don?

Martha grins. 'Very funny; you know damn well that 'joe' is an American term for coffee. You're winding me up.'

'Guilty as charged. But my Benny would love this place, and the owners even named it after him. He could have a franchise, in Clapham.' On the way out of the diner, Doris kisses a life-size cardboard cut-out of John Wayne.

'Be careful, your husband will get jealous,' says Martha.

Replete and refreshed, they cruise on, and the limo finally arrives at Silver Spur, and turns into a long straight drive, canopied by majestic oak trees. The visitors are awed by the size and beauty of the ranch land and love the elegant rustic simplicity of the timber house. It's so Martha.

'It's enormous, look at all that land,' says Doris.

Martha laughs. 'I thought the same when I first arrived, but apparently, it's tiny for Texas.'

None of them has met Don before, and when he introduces himself, they see what attracted Martha. He is ruggedly good looking and exudes genuine charm and open friendliness.

'It's wonderful to meet you all. My future wife doesn't stop singing your praises. We'll catch up at the wedding, but now I have to leave. My oldest friend has organised a bachelor party, and I'm being stabled back here early on the morning of the wedding. As we say here, I'll probably look like I was ridden hard and put away wet. I hope Martha will still have me!'

After the hen night

THE FRIENDS ARE GLAD they left a full day to recover, after the hen night. Despite good intentions, they all over-indulged. It's after eleven when they appear downstairs the next morning, everyone staggering straight to the coffee pot.

They ditch Martha's plan to show them some local sights after they take a vote. Doris wants to go back to Benny's to eat burgers and revisit John Wayne, but the others outvote her, preferring to rest on the terrace.

'I'm quite enjoying the local sights right here, thanks very much,' says Portia. 'Some of those ranch hands I see in the distance could make a fortune advertising jeans. I wish I'd brought my binoculars.'

THE HIGHLIGHT OF THE hen night was Doris getting up on a table to sing 'Achy Breaky Heart'. She got a standing ovation and followed it up with 'Islands in the Stream'.

When she got down from the table, Martha said, 'Wow, Doris that was incredible. That's the first time I've seen you sing holding a microphone instead of a duster or vacuum cleaner.'

'Get off with you,' Doris said, looking pleased.

Today they all agree they can't remember a more fun night out.

'But I could have killed you all when that cowboy asked me for a dance and then stripped down to a thong,' says Martha. 'How did you organise it, from back in England?'

'You're forgetting I know Simon,' says Doris. 'I got him to arrange things; he owed me a favour after all the clearing up I did after him. There was some confusion at first because nobody knew what he was on about: A hen night is a bachelorette party over here.'

'That's right, Doris. But I'm mortified, fancy asking my son, how embarrassing. I'll get my own back. I took a photo of you singing on the table. I'll send a copy to *your* son.'

'Do that, and I'll get Barry Brillo onto you: If anyone can dig up a scandal, he can. I'm glad we're relaxing today. There's so much to catch up on.'

'Too right,' says Martha. 'I have a surprise for you all. Come and help me, Doris, if you wouldn't mind.'

When they disappear into the house, Carlotta asks Portia, 'How's it all going. Are you happy?'

'Yes, I'm enjoying life. The store is hard work, but I love it. And I like living on my own, in my cute new house in Battersea, although I still haven't unpacked all the boxes. I met a dishy Italian man when I was on a buying trip to Rome a year ago. We see each other about once a month. Nothing serious, but it's fun. How about you, are you happy, do you still enjoy the Crempog?'

Carlotta pulls a face. 'It's OK, but Nerys employed a chef recently, Rick, and they only have eyes for each other. I feel like a gooseberry. And because of the chef, she's changed the way she runs the cafe. I preferred it when it was more like a tea shop. My column has been a success though. I'm thinking of adding to it and turning it into a book. What about you, Izzie? How's the Second Chance Club going?'

'It's going, literally. My Malibu friends are selling the beach house and moving to London for a few years, and I need to vacate the headquarters. I see it as a sign to move on, at least for a while, do something different, or maybe the same thing in a different place. I never thought I would hear myself say this, but I'd like a break from London.'

'Are you sure you won't miss it? I would certainly miss you,' says Portia.

'Sometimes it's good to have a change. I don't agree with what Samuel Johnson said: *When a man is tired of London he's tired of life,* I'm keeping an open mind; I still have the last of the family diamonds so I can afford to kick back for a while.'

'I thought Oscar Wilde said that?' says Portia.

'What, that I still have the family diamonds? Only joking, I know what you meant. I thought it was Wilde who said it, too, until the other day when I was browsing in Bookworms. Samuel said it way back in 1777 when he was chatting with his Scottish friend Boswell, who was wondering if the zest he felt for London would wane if he moved there full-time, rather than popping down from Edinburgh for holidays. Although, it wouldn't have been a 'pop' in those days; must have taken ages. My bum feels numb just thinking about it.'

Carlotta brings them back to the present. I'm excited for you, Izzie, although I hope you don't move too far away from us all. Oh, look Martha and Doris are heading this way. What on earth have they got in those huge boxes?'

'What have we missed? You were as thick as thieves when we came out,' says Martha.

'Never mind that, we'll tell you in a minute. What's in the packages?' asks Carlotta.

'Some fun stuff.'

They tear open the parcels, like kids on Christmas morning, to reveal cowboy hats and boots.

'They're great, are we off to a rodeo?' says Doris.

Martha clears her throat. 'I'm wearing cowboy boots and a Stetson with my wedding dress. I wondered if you'd all like to do the same, with your outfits, in real western wedding style. I won't be offended if you hate the idea.'

'How did you know what sizes to get us?' asks Portia.

'Remember when we went to Happy Soles? We spent ages trying on boots, and somehow I recalled your sizes. I hope I got it right. As for the hats, I took a wild guess. Try them on.'

Minutes later, Doris, Izzie, Carlotta and Portia are parading around the pool, pretending to be models. The boots and hats fit perfectly, and they agree it will be great fun to wear them to the wedding.

Doris is a little concerned how they will go with her pink chiffon frock, but she's game for a laugh. Izzie thinks it's a great idea. Portia is secretly disappointed she won't be wearing the hat she had specially made, by the Hanna Sasque Hat Company. However, she saves the word no for essential matters and prefers to say *yes* if it's easily doable and makes others happy. Nothing in the world would induce her to reduce the wattage of Martha's radiant smile.

Wedding belles

ON THE MORNING OF THE wedding, everyone is up later than planned, the night before was too much fun to wind it up early, and no one got to bed until after two. The girls went out to dinner then onto a millennium firework display. Doris watched from the car: 'I'm terrified of fireworks after one of those helicopter thingies chased me around our backyard and into the kitchen when I was six.'

Don had wanted fireworks at the wedding reception, but Martha refused; her trusty steed, Trigger had once gone wild with terror on 5th November, and she wouldn't risk upsetting the horses.

Martha is first in the dining room, followed by Izzie ten minutes later.

Gradually everyone appears. Doris looks adorable in a pink quilted flowered dressing-gown, still in her curlers. She is uneasy, watching the wedding organisers setting up and wants to help. Martha and Izzie tell her off, she's on holiday.

The sun warms up, and they move to the terrace, expecting the time to drag until it's time to put on their glad-rags, but there is so much to talk about they end up rushing to get dressed in time for the ceremony.

And what a ceremony it is; unpretentious, straightforward and heart-warming.

Martha looks divine in a gold silk, full-skirted dress, on the knee, worn with brown velvet cowboy boots and a gold Stetson. After the vows are said, the DJ plays John Prine and Iris Dement's 'In Spite of Ourselves', Don's and Martha's favourite.

The reception is a far cry from some of the stuffy affairs the girls have attended in England. There are no planned speeches, but a few impromptu ones. Don's is the best. He brings tears to everyone's eyes when he talks about falling in love at first sight with the beautiful woman on a horse.

The reception is cosy and convivial, with fifty guests. And the barbecue is delicious, with something for everyone, including plenty of vegetarian options. Wolf would approve. The choice of drinks is champagne, beer, bourbon, iced-tea, lemonade or water.

The girls love meeting Martha's mum and stepdad who are staying in Grand Star, a local hotel. Martha's dad was an American GI in the war who fell in love with Martha's mum, a Londoner, and they married and settled down in Sussex, taking most of their holidays in America. When Martha's dad died, ten years ago, her mum went to live in Los Angeles, and fell in love and got married again soon afterwards

'Why have you never told us much about your mum?' asks Doris. 'I love her, she's fun, and your stepdad is a sweetie, not to mention a bit of a silver fox.'

'We sort of fell out when I married James. Mum and Dad were against it and knew he was a bad egg, I should have listened, but I was too busy being impressed with James's fake flattery. Mum and I only fully reconciled since I've been over here. She loves my new hubby.'

THEY DANCE, THEY CHAT, and they laugh. In a day packed with joy and fun, nobody thinks there is room for any more surprises. They're wrong.

Soon it is after midnight. The band is mainly playing slow songs. Carlotta and Simon sit with Martha and her new husband.

Simon puts an arm around Martha. 'It's been a lovely day, Mum. I'm so happy for you both. I don't want to rain on your parade, but we want to tell you something. Don't worry; it's an idea you'll like. Carlotta and I want to be together.'

Martha might explode with happiness. It feels right, apart from a nagging doubt. She finally feels the way she's always wanted to about her son and doesn't want him to go and live back in the UK. Nor would she discourage him. She crosses her fingers. 'Does that mean you'll both live in Wales?'

Carlotta is a little embarrassed. 'I don't want to be presumptuous, Martha and Don but I've been discussing it with Simon, and he said there's always so much to do on the ranch, and never enough staff. I wonder if I could work here and write a novel in my spare time? I can bake, cook and clean. I'd need to go back to Wales for a few weeks to tie-up loose ends, break the news to Mum and Dad, and rent out the house.'

Martha's mind is whirling; she loves the idea but sees one small snag. 'It all sounds great. But what will you do about a work permit? I'm too much of a stickler to pay you in cash, off the books; you'd need to be official. I endured years of anxiety with James bending the rules and can't live through it again.'

Simon laughs. 'I know you, Mum, and I've thought of that. I was saving the best until last. As you know, I'm an American citizen. We're off to Vegas as soon as you leave for the Caribbean - we're getting married!'

'Hurrah!' shouts Scarlet. 'I was meant to be going to Thailand to reunite with Mum, but I'm not missing this.'

'Vegas here we come!' shouts Izzie. 'Can we all change our plans?'

There is a unanimous *yes* from everyone except Martha, who looks at Don.

'The Caribbean can wait, Martha.'

'I knew I did the right thing when I agreed to marry you, Mr O'Hara'

Epilogue

THE DAY BEFORE THEY all leave for Vegas Izzie phones London. She left the diamonds with a well-established company in Hatton Garden for an appraisal before Christmas, and it's their first day back. Waiting to be put through, Izzie wonders how much the jewels are worth and can't believe she hasn't checked before, but life has been a whirlwind. And she hasn't needed the money; almost as if she was on a magic carpet ride through life.

Izzie hears Mr Stone clearing his throat at the other side of the world. 'Hello, Miss Firecracker. Did you have any idea of the valuation before you left them with us?'

'A million pounds, at least.'

'I'm afraid it's a lot less.'

'How much are they worth?'

'Five thousand pounds: They're good copies of a set I valued a few years ago which was worth a small fortune.'

'Are you sure mine are fake?'

'I'm certain. You can come and pick the, ahem, jewels up at your convenience.'

Izzie redials; a London number.

'Hello, Belgrave House, Lady Loveday speaking.'

'Hello, I'm Izzie, Crispin's ex-wife. Can I have a word with your husband, please?'

'I'll get him. He's in the garage, polishing cars.'

'Now, there's a surprise, Lady Loveday.'

Izzie hears a tinkling laugh, followed by, 'Please, call me Loveday. Pop over for a drink some time. I'd love to meet you. We'd have asked you to our wedding, but I insisted on a quiet and private affair, didn't want the press haranguing us. Hang on, and I'll call him to the phone.'

After a short while, Izzie hears Crispin's voice. 'Hello, Izzie. What a pleasant surprise. Have you called for a reason, or for a chat?'

'It's about the diamonds.'

'I've been waiting for this day.'

'Then you knew?'

'Of course: You know how fond I am of a practical joke. The 'jewels' were copies of Mum's favourite set, which paid for most of the death duties. I can't believe you took so long to find out. What have you been living on?'

'On my wits and the kindness of God, the Universe or whatever you want to call it: I thought I was in a great situation, so I was.'

Crispin laughs. 'You know I'd always help you out if you were stuck. I thought you'd get back to me within days, weeks, months maybe, but not years.'

'You owe me dinner, Crispin - and maybe at least one proper diamond.' Believing she owned genuine diamonds had made Izzie feel financially safe; she must keep the feeling of inner security going, whatever the outer circumstances.

'Done, Izzie, dinner will be lovely. It will be good to catch up.'

Izzie ends the call. He'd only said dinner would be lovely. Diamonds would be too, but she isn't counting on them. She focuses on now, knowing everything will fall into place if she has trust.

It's time to pack for Vegas.

The End (Sort of)

If you want to enjoy Izzie's crazy and romantic adventures in Las Vegas, next in this series is *Movies, Mothers and Murder...*

Did you love *Izzie Firecracker and the Last of the Family Diamonds*? Then you should read *Movies, Mothers and Murder*[1] by Janet Butler Male!

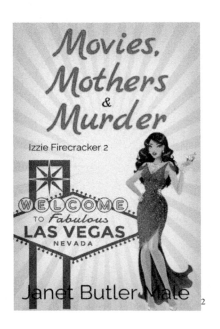

Out of the London frying pan into the Vegas fire

Zany London-based self-help guru, Izzie Firecracker, is broke due to a failed investment. She has to vacate her luxury home and office. Pronto. To add insult to injury, her mum goes and dies.

Izzie is at her lowest ever ebb when a drop-dead-handsome man, Bobby, telephones. He wants her in Las Vegas to run a self-help seminar in his decadent new hotel. It's a no-brainer.

1. https://books2read.com/u/4XKw16

2. https://books2read.com/u/4XKw16

Soon, Izzie and Bobby are at the mercy of Fingers Angelini...a mad mobster, out for blood -- and therapy.

Can Izzie and Bobby outwit the crazy gangster and escape with their lives, never mind their budding relationship?

A zany romantic comedy/suspense sprinkled with heaps of dark humour. Fasten your seatbelt for a fast, crazy ride.

Read more at www.janetbutlermale.co.uk.

Printed in Great Britain
by Amazon